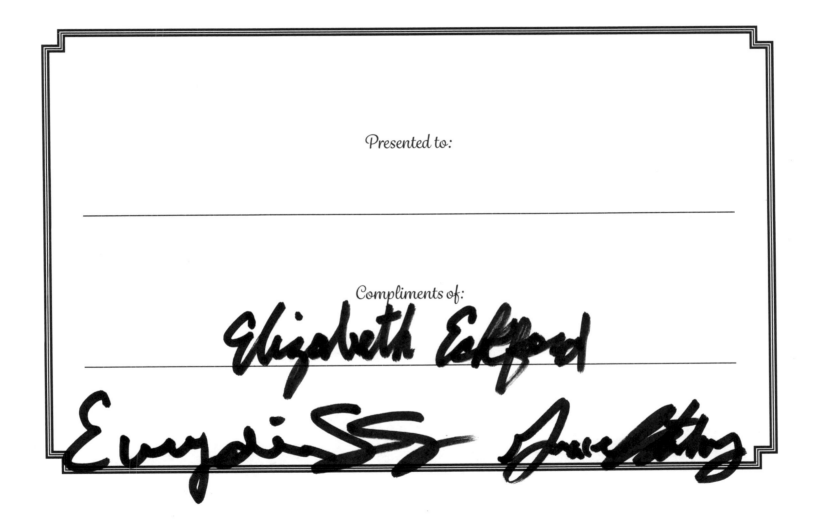

Presented to:

_____

Compliments of:

Elizabeth Eckford

The Worst First Day: Bullied While Desegregating Central High

This book is a publication of
Lamp Press, LLC
901 S. Old Corry Field Road #16325 • Pensacola FL 32507-6325
http://www.lamppressbooks.com

For bulk orders, speaker requests and general information, call (612) 888-7934 or email info@lamppressbooks.com.

First Edition: December 2017

Cataloging information for this book is available from the Library of Congress.

ISBNs – 978-0-9997661-0-1 (softcover), 978-0-9997661-1-8 (hardback) 978-0-9997661-2-5 (ebook)

Designed by Thomas Cunningham IV of BaileyCunningham & Company, Inc.
Foreword by Dr. Sybil Hampton
Edited by JoAnne French Kinkade
Cover Graphic Illustration by Rachel Gibson
Back Cover Photography Kirk Stephen Jordan

THE WORST FIRST DAY:

Bullied While Desegregating Central High

An Illustrated Autobiography

By Elizabeth Eckford, Member of the Little Rock Nine
with Dr. Eurydice and Grace Stanley

Foreword by Dr. Sybil Jordan Hampton
Graphic Artwork by Rachel Gibson

Photography by Will Counts and Kirk Jordan

Lamp Press, LLC

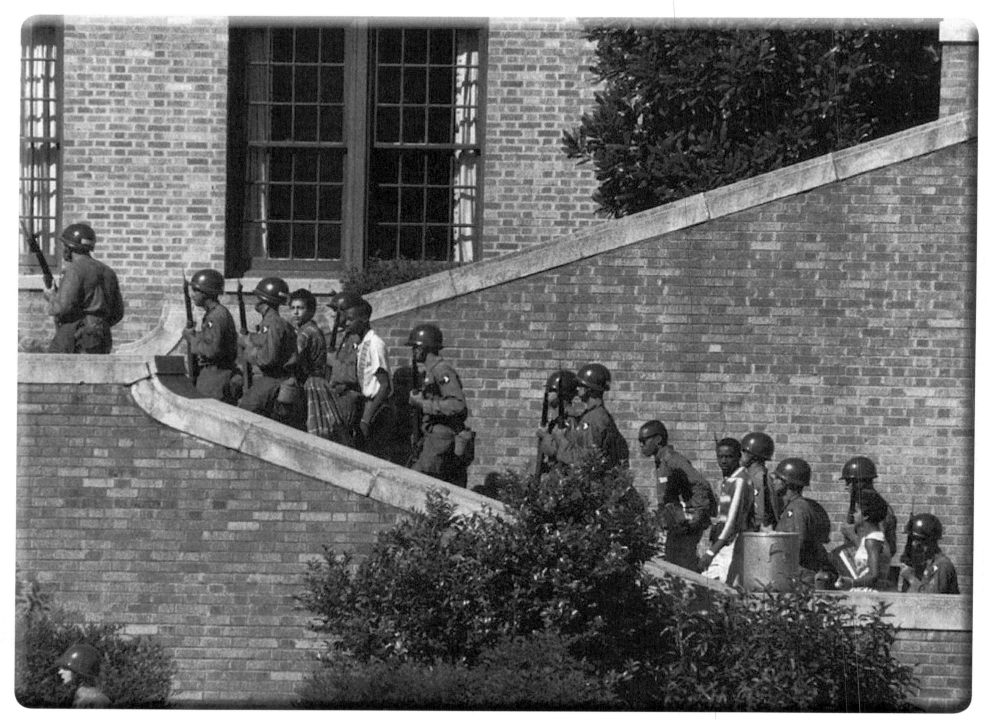

Contents

The Little Rock Nine Congressional Gold Medal

Dedication

To the avid young reader.
—Elizabeth

In loving memory of our favorite historian, Quewanncoii C. Stephens, II and our absolute heart, Aaron O. Weiss. Thank you both for loving us without limit. We miss you every single day.
—Eurydice & Grace

Introduction
Walking in Nine Footsteps
Dr. Sybil Jordan Hampton

You hold in your hands the incredible account of an unlikely heroine. In 1957, Elizabeth Eckford simply attempted to go to school at Central High. By the next morning, she became the most recognized teen in the world. Well before the phrase "go viral" was coined, images of Elizabeth's attempts to enter Central High, thwarted by segregationists and soldiers, made international headlines. The world was shocked and outraged, with good reason.

Elizabeth's story is a compelling, modern-day "Odyssey" set during the civil rights era. This book plants seeds of courage in the readers' hearts, compelling them to build their resilience and follow Elizabeth's example when surrounded by chaos. Like me, the world remained in awe of the stoic girl who walked through a lion's den without stooping to the level of her attackers. Elizabeth was an example then, and remains one now.

I am grateful to be part of the second group of African American students to attend Central High School. It was an honor to walk in the footsteps of Elizabeth and the Little Rock Nine. The Central High Crisis remained international news for several years. Everyone in Little Rock clearly understood the significance of what was happening at the school. I attended Central with great anticipation, in the hopes of continuing the important work the "Nine" had begun.

The Central High Crisis was a conflict between the state and the federal government. The south has always been adamant that states' rights trump the federal government, as evidenced by the Civil War. Initially, the state rejected the 1954 Brown v. the Board of Education decision to desegregate schools. The Central conflict was very important, because it reflected shame for our state and nation. It was the first major racial incident televised. The entire country witnessed what happened in Little Rock, including the lack of response by many white citizens who stood by idly while watching the mayhem.

Governor Orval Faubus shut down Central High after the Little Rock Nine survived their first year. He was willing to do just about anything to keep African American students out of "his" schools. His racism kept the schools closed for a year. They were only reopened under court order and after extensive legal battles.

Central High reopened in 1959. There were only five African American students allowed into the school that year. The students were Frank Henderson, Saundra Johnson, myself and two of the original Little Rock Nine, Carlotta Walls and Jefferson Thomas. The Little Rock School Board used a process that was anchored by the pupil placement law. I was recruited as a candidate due to my involvement with the NAACP Youth Council and activities in my church and school. The Little Rock Nine's experiences influenced the School Board to change its selection process. We underwent extensive screening including psychological and intelligence testing. If we passed that round, we were interviewed by the Little Rock School Board, which was all-male and all-white. They made the final selections.

Although I was aware of the horrible things that happened to the Nine, I decided to go to Central anyway. It was an incredible opportunity. However, I found that opposition to the new group of African American students attending Central was manifested in a different way than the

> *You hold in your hands the incredible account of an unlikely heroine.*

brutal experiences of the original Nine. We were shunned, ignored as if we did not exist. As an active, lively child, I never thought that such a thing could happen, but I kept a stiff upper lip. I remained focused on my goal, which was to desegregate Central High, be successful as a student and to avoid harm.

Their actions were startling. I was an active, lively student who was never shunned before in my life. I was someone who was deeply involved in school and church. The possibility of being shunned never entered my mind, but I had no idea of what would happen. When it did, I put my head down and did what I needed to do. But inside I felt very sad, though not alone. I went to Central with the right expectations because I saw what the Nine endured. I was walking in their footsteps.

As I watched the example set by the Nine, they mentored me. I believe the lessons learned in this book can initiate a dialogue and critical messages that have been lost over time. Life is not always fair! Few would be able to endure the existence that we did, especially in high school, but we knew what we did was for a far greater purpose than making new friends. The Little Rock Nine had the same vision, and I encourage parents and caregivers to instill that sense of direction in their youth so that they can stand during tough times.

Sybil Jordan as a Central High student

Racism is an evil thing. I thought over time that the students at Central would want to get to know me as a person, but they discounted everything about me due to the color of my skin. They did not have any desire to recognize my "sameness" with them. The prejudice they learned from their ancestors forced them to completely cut themselves off from me for something that I had no control over.

Parents, it is so important for you to read this book and discuss it with your children. The most important thing in my life was my upbringing. In the segregated environment in which I grew up, parents remained actively engaged with their children to ensure they would be safe. They taught their children "the rules" of segregation and how to respect the rules to keep them from harm until there would be a time when those rules would no longer impact us.

We were brought up to understand that there were colored water fountains and colored bathrooms for a reason. I knew that I was not going to have a Coca-Cola in Woolworth's or Rexall drug store, not with segregation. Similarly, I was not going to waltz into a movie theatre and sit anyplace I wanted to watch a movie. I knew that I would have to sit in the balcony, and I would have to enter most establishments through the back door.

That was the nature of segregation and the reality of the era. It was not very long ago, and it continues to impact us to this day. It was not as if the Nine had their first experiences with discrimination at Central. Growing up in a segregated system, people of color were subjected to countless instances of rejection or injustice every day. Our parents taught us to live with what is, and to prepare for what will be.

From the time of slavery, our people in this country always believed that there would be a generation that enjoyed all the promises of democracy. When I was a child, ours was believed to be that generation. Therefore, education was very important. We were encouraged to become educated and do the best we could because we may be the first one of our people to truly have more opportunities in society than anyone has ever had since slavery. We were like a hydra-headed monster – we lived the promises of the future.

Parents, you can plant the seeds of success in your children. Youth, take lessons learned from what Elizabeth Eckford and the Little Rock Nine lived through and become resilient. Persevere. Surround the youth in your community with love to ensure that they are confident.

Although the desire is to protect children as much as possible, we must balance that feeling with knowledge. Struggle is global, and it is not limited to one single group or race. If we want to insure our children's success we must help them understand the concept of sacrifice. Attending Central

High tried the Little Rock Nine by fire. They were willing to do what was necessary to blaze a trail for the students who followed. We were as well.

Those of us who went to the school knew we had to turn the other cheek when outrageous things were said to us, because we did not want to become engulfed in hate. We did not want to lose our moral center, or foundations of faith, or our ability to be loving and forgiving, because that was who we were. My ability to love and forgive was never compromised. My parents showed me that doing well was the best revenge. So I did not concede on my personal values, my wonderful mind, my ability to be a good student, good citizen and good person. I was grateful to walk in the footsteps of nine young civil rights soldiers who opened the door for me.

In turn, I held the door for the next group. Hopefully, I was able to encourage someone else to stand up and be counted. To students who are struggling or being bullied in school today, know that you are not alone. Stand tall, and stay encouraged.

Dr. Sybil Jordan Hampton today.

Foreward
By Elizabeth Eckford

It has been 60 years since I first attempted to attend Central High. For those who wonder why I share my story now, the reason is simple…I feel as though I must. People are being harassed in toxic environments at school and work. They endure hateful statements from their peers with no reprieve in sight. Some people don't understand the consequence of what they say and do. I sincerely hope that by sharing my story, I can make them start recognizing the impact of their behavior.

For years, I internalized my feelings from the torment I was forced to undergo at Central High simply because I desired a better education and a better future. I didn't start speaking in public about what happened until 1996, after I was reunited with the only two white students who were compassionate towards me at school - Kendall Reinhart and Ann Williams. I saw them at a Central High reunion, and felt that it was important for them to know that they saved my life through kindness.

Kendall and Ann were the only students in the entire school who spoke to me when some attacked me verbally, physically, and most of all, mentally. Unfortunately, children in schools are still being hounded by bullies, and the consequences can be deadly. Suicide is on the rise nationally. Those increases have been attributed to bullying.

The act of bullying can never be justified. It is more a reflection of the attacker than the person being attacked. However, that truth can be difficult to recognize while one suffers through the demeaning process of being bullied.

I want students to realize the power in their words.

Telling Ken and Ann how grateful I was to them for what they did for me was freeing! After meeting them, I started accepting speaking requests to share my experiences at Central High with the hopes of inspiring others to be kind and stand up for their peers. There were more speaking engagements after Little Rock had its first city-wide recognition of Central High's desegregation in 1997, honoring the 40th anniversary. Although I understood the importance of sharing my story, every time I spoke about what happened I would end up in tears.

Thankfully, I don't cry anymore.

The Civil Rights Movement was accomplished by everyday citizens in their local communities who were taking big chances. They often put their lives at risk unexpectedly, especially those who fought for voting rights. The year prior to my attending Central High, I was inspired by the unity of the African American community during the Montgomery Bus Boycott, lasting from 1955-1956. The community united, refusing to take public transportation after Rosa Parks was jailed for refusing to ride in the back of the bus as dictated by Jim Crow laws and segregation.

As citizens refused public transportation by walking or carpooling to work, Montgomery finally conceded. That is the power of unity, a power that must be tapped again if we have any hopes of turning the current tides that seem to want to send us back to times of segregation and racial division. Standing together is our only hope.

Sharing what I endured at Central High has had a healing effect. I gain strength and energy from the students and adults that I have had the honor to speak with, and encourage others to speak their truth. Although I am still impacted by the deliberately hateful, life-altering attacks that I suffered at Central High, I recognize my progress every day, as do my family and friends. Twenty years after I started speaking about this issue, I am almost a completely different person today, and I am grateful.

I want students to realize the power in their words. They can bring change by supporting someone who is being harassed. They can ensure others know they aren't despised due to different characteristics that simply do not matter, including race. It is important to know that you can be a hero to others by supporting them. That is a sure-fire way to minimize the impact of bullies, and build up the hearts and minds of those who have been harassed.

I am proud to share my story. The book you now hold is a dream many years in the making. I hope that this information helps someone else. Most importantly, know that you are not alone. It is my hope that no one will have to carry the burden of racism ever again.

THE WORST FIRST DAY:

Bullied While Desegregating Central High

On the first day of school, I gazed at my new dress with pride.
My sister Anna helped me make it out of the prettiest material we could find.
The blouse was white with a sleek collar and the skirt had navy blue gingham trim,
Today I would integrate an all-white school, and I wanted to look my best for them!

My mind raced as I prepared for school rejoicing over this incredible opportunity.
Like most students, I was both nervous and excited about my first day.
No one could imagine how important my new school was to me.
I never suspected I would soon endure an attack that would change my life in countless ways!

The date was September 4, 1957, a time when everything was segregated except local busses.
Under segregation, people of color and white people did not mix.
Given the beauty of today's diverse, multi-cultural world,
I'm sure it is hard for you to imagine this!

HISTORY NOTE

The Fourteenth Amendment to the Constitution provides protections for all American citizens. In 1896, the Supreme Court case Plessy v. Ferguson contested desegregation. The case was lost, legalizing "equal but separate" services nationwide. Essentially the judges did not believe equal protections meant races sitting collectively. "Jim Crow" laws institutionalized state enforced discrimination. Also during this time, miscegenation codes prevented marriage of whites with people of color including Asians, Africans, Hispanics, and Native Americans. They also banned any interracial children.

Little Rock schools mirrored state segregation laws.

Only white schools received new books and the best school facilities.

Black schools received "hand-me-down," written-in books and decrepit resources,

With limited resources, our teachers worked harder to teach us to write and read.

In 1954, five families had enough, suing the school boards for their children's future.

They wanted their students to have access to equal education and real opportunity.

Their cases were combined with Oliver and Linda Brown, forming Brown v. the Board of Education.

The Supreme Court case was skillfully led by Thurgood Marshall and lawyers from the NAACP.

[No State shall] deny to any person within its jurisdiction the equal protection of the laws.

Fourteenth Amendment

The defense introduced unique testimony to the court,
Proving the long-term impact of discrimination on young minds.
Evidence included the "Doll Test," research by psychologist Drs. Kenneth and Mamie Clark,
When asked, "Which Doll Is Good?" black children chose the white doll, almost every time.

The abundance of evidence proved discrimination detrimentally impacted a child's self-esteem.
Marginalized school facilities ensured black students received much less.
Due to their diligence in court and thorough litigation,
Thurgood Marshall's exceptional team achieved success!

Although the Supreme Court decision ruled in favor of educational diversity,
It took years for many school boards to implement the court's rulings.
If integration was of a financial benefit to the county, it took place almost instantly,
As was the case for the small nearby town of Hoxie.

Thurgood Marshall representing the Little Rock Nine in one of many court appearances.

In 1955, the small town of Hoxie integrated 21 African American students in elementary school.

Their superintendent of schools said the move was "right in the sight of God," and would save money.

Photos of their integrated classrooms published in Life magazine caused an uproar from outside racists.

They staged protests until the Department of Justice authorized the FBI to intervene.

Desegregation was taking too long to reach Little Rock, so Cooper v. Aaron was filed in 1956.

Attorney Wiley Branton sued the Little Rock School Board on behalf of black families.

The case attempted to force the city to follow the Brown decision and initiate desegregation,

By not enforcing the ruling, the state rebuffed the Supreme Court as the law of the land daily.

 HISTORY NOTE

Some small towns that did not have high schools had to transport black students to segregated schools in larger towns. It could be quite expensive to transport and even house students in neighboring towns. Apparently, integration was much more readily accepted when it was financially beneficial to the community.

Elizabeth and her mother Birdie

Little Rock's school integration was eventually outlined in the "Blossom Plan".

Although the plan claimed to be color-blind, it enforced residential segregation lines within our community.

Superintendent of Schools Virgil Blossom planned to start desegregation in the high schools.

Then, over the next six years, integration would branch out to the lower grades eventually.

We were told about the opportunity to attend Central during the Spring of 1957.

I called my Mother, Birdie Eckford, "The Queen of No" because she was extremely protective of me.

She surprised me, however, while contemplating my request to attend Central.

Instead of immediately saying no, she simply replied, "We'll see."

Black student applicants submitted academic transcripts and were subjected to several interviews.

Blossom whittled more than 200 initial African American Central High applicants down to 17.

However, when the names of the first students selected were listed in the newspaper,

Several applicants dropped out due to community threats, pressure and scrutiny.

My name was not published in the papers because I had not yet been interviewed or selected.

My parents were very slow to approve my request to attend Central initially.

Had my name been printed, my parents probably would have felt pressure on their jobs,

But Grandpa would not have cared because he ran his own neighborhood grocery store independently.

Although I wanted to attend Central, the thought of integrating the school made me nervous,

But I was extremely happy when told I made the "integration team".

Superintendent Blossom made it clear he didn't want any "troublemakers".

But I was quiet, shy, and never got in trouble...I knew his concerns did not apply to me.

Most of the families selected were middle class, but my parents worked two jobs each.

My Father worked split-shift for Missouri Pacific Railroad and on staff for three rich families.

My Mother served in a laundry and as a maid to ensure we were able to meet our basic needs.

My five siblings and I knew our parents worked hard because they loved us unconditionally.

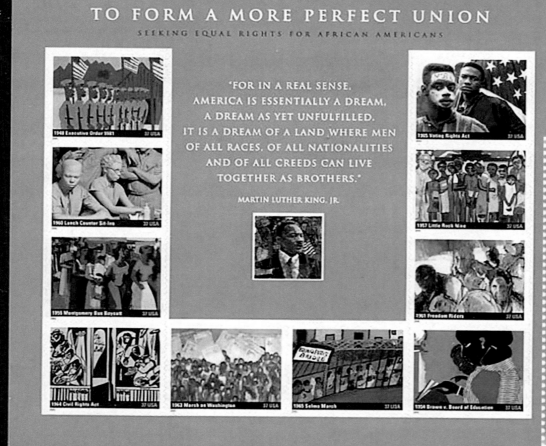

The Little Rock Nine were featured as part of a 2005 commemorative stamp set representing key moments in the Civil Rights movement.

This was the era of the civil rights movement, when African Americans waged war against segregation and racism.
In 1955, Rosa Parks refused to give up her seat in the "whites only" section on a public bus as she did in the past.[1]
Her subsequent arrest sparked the Montgomery Bus Boycott, lasting thirteen months,
When African Americans refused to financially support public transit, the segregationist system crashed!

The Montgomery Bus Boycott was heavily influenced by Dr. Martin Luther King, Jr.
He was a dynamic Civil Rights leader who led by example in the quest for equality.
He encouraged youth to participate in the movement, demanding non-violent practices.
A Pastor, Dr. King believed that love and a sincere sense of "we" was the way to racial unity.

The Brown vs. Board of Education verdict meant an end to "separate but equal" schools.
Unequal schools were blatantly recognizable in Little Rock teaching disparities.
Education for students of color was considered industrial, or skilled labor capacities.
Students were taught skills such as bricklaying, auto repair, printing, typing and carpentry.

HISTORY NOTE

My previous school was funded by Julius Rosenwald, philanthropist and Chairman of the Board of Sears, Roebuck & Company. He built nearly 5,000 schools for black students in an unequal educational system that was purposefully constrained. At the turn of the century, nearly one third of the South's black children attended a one-room, wooden Rosenwald school, his altruism filled a substantial gap until the Brown decision forced schools to integrate.

Minnijean Brown
16-year-old junior

Elizabeth Eckford
15-year-old junior

Ernest Green
16-year-old senior

Thelma Mothershed
16-year-old junior

Melba Pattill
15-year-old jun

Rosenwald built my former school named in honor of poet Paul Lawrence Dunbar.

Booker T. Washington collaborated with Rosenwald, so our curriculum modeled his Institute in Tuskegee.

My Dunbar classmates would become known as "The Little Rock Nine," but we started with ten

Thelma Mothershed, Melba Patillo Beals, Jefferson Thomas, Ernest Green, Minnijean Brown,
   Carlotta Walls, Terrence Roberts, Gloria Ray, Jane Hill and me.

Though we went to the same school, some of us hardly knew one another.

The students selected were mostly tenth and eleventh graders with one senior, Ernest Green.

Previously, we attended segregated schools such as Dunbar and Horace Mann high school.

The Little Rock Nine was advised by Mrs. Daisy Bates, President of the local NAACP.

Gloria Ray
15-year-old junior

Terrence Roberts
15-year-old junior

Jefferson Thomas
15-year-old sophomore

Carlotta Walls
14-year-old sophomore

18

I was elated to attend Central High because it was such a prestigious institution.

It was state-of-the-art and the most impressive school to be found.

Central cost more than $1.5 million dollars to build in 1927,

An expense that would be more than 20 million dollars now!

Central High architects won numerous awards for its artistic design.

They even designed Gothic statues to welcome students every morning over the front door.

Each statue had a name such as Ambition, Personality, Preparation, and Opportunity.

To me, the pillars represented the endless possibilities my new school had in store!

Potential risks were identified to the Nine, but no one could predict the horrors we faced.

We knew there would be sacrifices as the first black students attending an all-white campus.

We were advised we couldn't participate in any of Central's after school activities.

Losing that option was no issue for me because Mother didn't approve of such activities for us.

However, it was quite a blow to the others because they were so active in their schools.

Jefferson was an exceptional athlete and Thelma was President of the National Honor Society.

Most of the Nine had talents, Ernest played saxophone in the band and Minnijean sang.

But since the sacrifice meant attending Central, the forfeit was made willingly.

Our families were spoken to disrespectfully by school administrators and leaders.

We clearly knew that if hit or harmed by a fellow student, we could never strike back.

We were expected to be submissive when faced with conflict; we had to bite our tongues and walk away.

We swallowed our pride to ensure future students would have the chance we previously lacked.

Few parents were happy that students of color would now attend Central High.

Segregationists protested this monumental change and sought legislative relief.

At first, Arkansas Governor Orval Faubus didn't care much about the issue one way or the other.

But when he realized the potential damage to his political future, he changed his beliefs.

On Labor Day, September 3, Governor Faubus' television address put segregationists in a frenzy.

He claimed threats of violence and was sending in the National Guard, inciting fear and infuriation.

He was well aware segregationists did not adhere to Dr. King's non-violent teachings or beliefs,

"Blood will run through the streets if negroes attempt to attend Central High", he predicted to the nation.

During this era, African Americans were called many derogatory slurs routinely.
Racial epithets are used to divide, separate, and undermine.
Terms such as "negro" and "colored" were used with Jim Crow laws to create racial castes.
When describing another human being, race should not be the way to define!

Faubus upset many protestors with his Labor Day address, so only white students attended school the first day.
Segregationist groups such as the Mothers' League and the Capital Citizens' Council had protestors ready anyway.
They held a sunrise prayer service and sang songs such as "Dixie" in front of Central High.
Some even donned Confederate outfits and espoused beliefs that blacks attempting to attend Central should die!

The second day, September 4 was my actual first day of school.
Large crowds were reported outside of Central High on TV.
My family and I prayed before I left that morning.
I was both anxious and nervous about what was to be.

The character of Jim Crow came to represent racial segregation during the era.

24

My father usually worked nights, but he stayed up that morning.

The parents of the Little Rock Nine were told not to escort their children to school.

As I prepared for my day, he paced the floor nervously.

Administrators hoped to reduce the possibility of conflict and hostility.

As I rode the bus to school, I felt that I was being transported to a whole new world.

With each inch that I moved closer, my dreams soared higher!

I wondered who'd be my new friends and if I received my desired classes from the school registrar.

Little did I know that I would soon be entering a cauldron of fire.

Exiting the bus, I pondered my bright new future as I walked the rest of the way to school.

Up ahead, I saw more than 250 people in a massive crowd.

They were quiet until I crossed the street to enter school, immediately sparking them to life.

Their initial quiet murmurings became enraged and extremely loud.

I was scared at first, but when I saw the armed soldiers I was relieved.

I thought they'd protect me from the angry mob screaming horrible things I couldn't believe!

Shouts included, "Go Home, @!&&+'/!" from mad, mean faces.

Could this hatred be simply because I wanted to go to school with different races?

I crossed the street to enter the school from the side.

But the Arkansas National Guard blocked my every try.

Three hundred Soldiers surrounded the school wearing battle fatigues and holding rifles in their arms.

I soon realized they weren't there to protect me, but I didn't understand why.

Soldiers allowed white students access to school from the front, so I thought I was in the wrong place.

But despite three separate attempts, I was never allowed entry.

Each time I was barred from entering the school, my anxiety increased,

Especially when the soldiers raised their weapons to block me.

I was terrified as I navigated between the soldiers and the angry crowd, wondering,

"Why is this happening? Can't anyone help?" I cried internally.

I saw an elderly lady who looked like a Grandma and hoped that she might assist.

But when I approached her to request help, she spat in my face promptly!

Several others in the crowd followed her filthy example between racial taunts and screams.

My mind raced, "How could you be so hateful? I'm only 15!"

I couldn't understand their behaving this way simply because I wanted to learn.

How could they despise me so much and say things so horribly cruel and mean?

Looking back, I was woefully unprepared for the adversity that I faced.

Prior to my first day of school, there were no meetings with Mrs. Bates or the NAACP.

When the Nine's plans, changed, I wasn't contacted because my family didn't have a phone.

As a result, I was alone when facing a racist mob that threatened to kill me!

While the crowd called me every racial epithet under the sun, I wondered,

"What if I were your daughter? Would you protect me then?"

I had never done anything to them and was only a junior in high school.

Yet they hated me because of the color of my skin!

I had so looked forward to this special day,

But now, all I wanted to do was go home.

I tried to find a way to escape,

But the crowd would not leave me alone!

To make matters worse, several girls followed me screaming horrible things.

I remained focused on trying to get home and never turned around.

One of the people hysterically screaming racial epithets was Hazel Bryan.

Despite their attack, I held my head high and from me she never heard a sound.

A young photographer named Will Counts captured images that morning of the attack.

He perfectly framed Hazel screaming in the crowd, identifying racial hatred for posterity.

His photo later became one of the most iconic images of the 20th century.

Counts was also nominated for a Pulitzer Prize in photography.

I heard taunts like "Two, four, six, eight, we don't want to integrate!" chanted by the mob.

Their preparations made me wonder how long they planned this assembly.

It was very clear to every participant, observer, and journalist in the crowd,

They neither approved of black students at their schools or race-mixing.

As I continued to navigate through the mob seeking a path of escape,

Several members yelled "Lynch her, lynch her!" and I took those threats seriously.

I remembered the heartbreaking photos published two years prior of 13-year-old Emmett Till's lynching.

His attackers tortured him to unrecognizability, and killed him for flirting with a white woman, allegedly.

34

Our community knew the accusation of Emmett being forward with the white woman was a malicious lie.

His Mother Mamie warned Emmett of the differences in mindsets before he left Chicago to visit relatives in Mississippi.

In 1955, Emmett's mother displayed his tortured body for the world to see what hatred and racism did to her baby.

The truth was finally revealed when Carolyn Bryant Donham confessed her lie in 2017.

Emmett's fate was readily on my mind while I tried to escape the massive throng.

From behind, I could hear the crowd, especially that group of girls, scream.

Hazel later said she was only copying her friend Sammie Dean Parker.

But the fame of Counts' photograph was due to capturing the hatred on her face – it radiated and beamed.

Let this be a lesson-be careful not to follow the wrong leader!

Like Hazel, you could succumb to negative influences and be the one who takes the blame.

The people you surround yourself with are essentially your reflection.

Had Hazel not followed that crowd, the world would never have known her name.

If a different photo had been selected, Hazel was not even seen.

Deciding to torment me with her friends changed both our lives in countless ways.

Support actions that help others, not hurt them.

Let your fame come from kindness or intelligence, not from inflicting pain.

I didn't notice Counts taking photographs because I was engulfed in the crowd.

I was scared out of my mind in a mass of hatred and revulsion that never seemed to end.

I saw the city bus stop on the corner and thought, "If I can only get there, I will be safe."

I don't know why that bench represented shelter, but somehow in my mind, it did.

The bus stop couldn't have been more than 100 feet away from the school,

But in that horde, attempting to reach the mark seemed like an impossibility.

With every step, my heart both sank and pounded loudly.

I tried to remain stoic and maintain my composure despite the vile attacks surrounding me.

I finally reached the bus stop exhausted as the crowd made evil plans, screaming "Drag her over to this tree!"

Thankfully, there were a few who tried to help, like Benjamin Fine, a New York Times reporter.

He had a daughter and embraced me protectively, saying, "Don't let them see you cry."

Several local reporters stood behind the bench to prevent anyone from striking me and maintain order.

I wore sunglasses because my eyes were sensitive to bright light and sunshine.
But that day, I was especially grateful for them because they helped hide my tears of pain.
While anticipating the bus arrival, I sat quietly, gathered my thoughts, and prayed the attack would end.
I focused on seeing my Mom and not allowing the bullies ever to see my tears again!

Two other valiant souls tried to intervene and help me avoid the threatening crowd,
But I knew my Mother wouldn't approve of me leaving with strangers, especially men.
I hadn't yet officially met Mr. L.C. Bates when he showed me his gun and said, "Come with me!"
I stayed on the bench because I believed my Mother would not want me to leave with him.

Years later, I understood my Mother was so protective because she sought to keep me safe.[2]
History recounts numerous atrocities against women of color, but I didn't initially understand her fears.
Slave owners routinely beat or lynched men and raped women considered their "property",
Unfortunately, the legacy of their warped mindsets validating vicious acts was passed down through the years.

Terrence Roberts arrived by himself to face the soldiers blocking Central.
He also wasn't notified of the Nine's change in plans and walked to school from his home nearby.
When Terrence saw my plight, he tried to help and offered to take me to his home for safety.
But I knew Mother wouldn't approve and I'd later still have to walk a mile home alone, so I didn't try.

"A Long Walk"
by Sophie King, Senior – Central High School
Little Rock Central High 1957-2007: Commemorating 50 years of Integration

40

Terrence and I graduated from 9th grade at Dunbar junior high together.

I had a crush on him when we were students because I thought he was cute.

Terrence seemed to be so confident and have such a strong sense of self.

Despite his youth, he valiantly tried to help me escape the swarm. He had my eternal gratitude.

I doubt I could have moved from that bench anyway because I was completely in shock.

I prayed for the next bus to arrive quickly to take me to my Mommy.

Then a kind woman, Mrs. Grace Lorch, stood by my side and tried to help me.

"You should be ashamed of yourselves," she screamed at the mob, protecting me like family.

Mrs. Lorch told the crowd that she hoped one day her little girl would attend school with negro children.

That statement from a white woman only made the crowd more incensed.

I couldn't believe how she was standing up to the mob on my behalf.

I never heard a white woman stand up for a colored child like this!

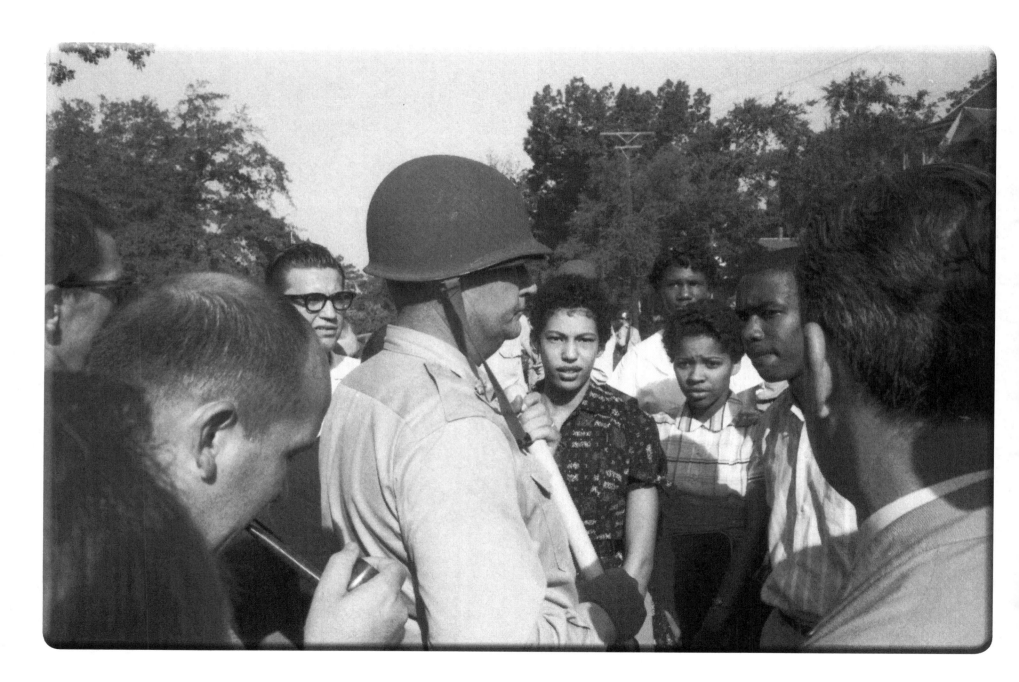

42

The rest of the Little Rock Nine arrived shortly thereafter with black and white clergy.

They too were prevented by the National Guard from entry.

Jane Hill, the other original African American student selected to attend Central,

Decided to return to Horace Mann after seeing the crowd's vicious frenzy!

The bus seemed to take an eternity, so I tried to call a cab from the drugstore across the street.

In the 1950s, we did not yet have the invention of cell phones.

However, the store owner locked the door, saying "I don't want any trouble."

Despite my bus stop protectors, I returned to the bench feeling anxious, scared and alone.

Half an hour later, the bus finally arrived and Mrs. Lorch joined me.

She and the bus driver prevented harassers from following me.

When I assured her I was fine, she got off the bus a few blocks away.

All I really wanted or needed at the time was my Mommy.

Arkansas National Guard riot club.

I was later told Mrs. Lorch's family was labeled as communists and blacklisted for trying to help,
Under "McCarthyism", anyone could be charged without proof with treason against America.
Her family was tormented with a cross burned on her lawn and their home was even bombed!
When her husband's position wasn't renewed, the Lorch family moved to Canada.

After jumping off the bus, I ran straight to the Arkansas School for the Negro Deaf and Blind.
Mom worked there in the laundry teaching students how to take care of their clothing.
I knew she was aware of what happened at Central because her head was bowed in prayer.
She hugged me tight without saying a word...that moment meant EVERYTHING to me!

During my first day at Central, I suffered hateful actions that could devastate a person's heart.
Later, I was overwhelmed by a media frenzy when images of the attack were published internationally.
Everyone had an opinion about what happened to me that day.
Commentary was heard from President Eisenhower, civil rights leaders and national celebrities.

The media attention from the photo was overwhelming.

I was interviewed or quoted every day.

It was hard to remain focused on being a student.

So many organizations pulled me in 50 different ways.

Newspapers covered the attack around the world.

There were headlines from France, Italy, and even Germany.

The only news story that receiving nearly as much coverage as our effort to desegregate Central

Was Russia launching Sputnik into outer space!

The international media coverage brought in countless letters of support from around the world.

If senders didn't know our names, they wrote Little Rock, USA or taped our pictures as addresses for delivery.

Supporters sent kind words to encourage the Little Rock Nine, denouncing discrimination and racism.

No one knew how important those messages were to my family and me!

— —

THE WHITE HOUSE

U. S. Naval Base
Newport, Rhode Island

THE PRESIDENT TODAY SENT THE
FOLLOWING TELEGRAM TO THE
HONORABLE ORVAL E. FAUBUS,
THE GOVERNOR OF ARKANSAS

The Honorable Orval E. Faubus
Governor of Arkansas
Little Rock, Arkansas

Your telegram received requesting my assurance of understanding
of and cooperation in the course of action you have taken on school
integration recommended by the Little Rock School Board and
ordered by the United States District Court pursuant to the mandate
of the United States Supreme Court.

When I became President, I took an oath to support and defend the
Constitution of the United States.   The only assurance I can give
you is that the Federal Constitution will be upheld by me by every
legal means at my command.

There is no basis of fact to the statements you make in your telegram
that Federal authorities have been considering taking you into custody
or that telephone lines to your Executive Mansion have been tapped
by any agency of the Federal Government.

At the request of Judge Davies, the Department of Justice is
presently collecting facts as to interference with or failure to
comply with the District Court's order.   You and other state
officials -- as well as the National Guard which, of course, is
uniformed, armed and partially sustained by the Government --
will, I am sure, give full cooperation to the United States District
Court.

                                        Dwight D. Eisenhower

Some countries used the Central Crisis to condemn racism in America.

A broadcast was even shared in Russian classrooms about my attempted first day.

Although many were embarrassed about the reports,

Unfortunately, they weren't embarrassed enough to make racism go away.

Political cartoonists made routine satire of the Central High Crisis.[3]

Governor Faubus was mocked for his segregationist actions against youth, his discriminatory views and political stance.

But his primary concern was his reelection campaign for Governor in 1958,

He believed without the segregationist vote, his campaign wouldn't have a chance.

Governor Faubus was later questioned about his inflammatory comments that incited racists.

The FBI wanted proof of the previously claimed threats attributed to segregationists.

He had the Arkansas National Guard protect his home from supposed threat,

Yet his comments incited his followers, even students, who would soon treat us like enemies and attack us.

President Eisenhower saw video footage of my attack and was infuriated.

He knew something must be done to make the Brown ruling last.

He awaited the response of the courts before stepping in.

He hoped to ensure separation of federal government and states as in the past.

The Nine was out of school for nearly three weeks after our first attempt.

In the interim, we completed assignments at Mrs. Bates' home to prevent falling behind.

Meanwhile, lawyers fought in court to uphold the Brown decision and return us back to school.

Despite many misgivings, we remained determined to ensure our dream of school diversity wasn't undermined.

Governor Faubus told President Eisenhower he would disperse the racist crowds.

But in truth, he continued to instigate segregationists and prey on their desire for racial exclusivity.

Numerous demonstrations took place while we were out of school.

They made it clear that "race-mixing" was something in which they did not believe.

On September 23, the Little Rock Nine attempted once again to attend Central High.
More than 1,000 segregationists awaited our arrival in a scene that was frantic and hectic.
Their attention was diverted to the end of the block near the Mobil service station.
As a result, we were able to sneak into Central through a side door undetected.

We discovered few were happy we made it to school.
Sammie Dean jumped out of a second story window to avoid us, while others tried to hide.
It was hard to believe that we were despised and hated this much because of racism.
Unfortunately, more hysterics were taking place outside.

We only remained in school a few hours before the mob realized we were inside.
The enraged crowd wanted to beat us or lynch us, they didn't care which.
The Police Chief instructed our escorts, "Drive and don't stop for anything,"
The officer who hid us under blankets in his car was so scared, he shook and twitched!

We later discovered the crowd was attacking three African American journalists when we arrived.

One was Alex Wilson, who served proudly during World War II as a Marine.

He was Editor of the Memphis Tri-State Defender and withstood a vicious attack without dropping his hat.

Despite being hit in the head with a brick, he maintained his dignity and refused to run from the scene.

Mr. Wilson's brutal assault was the final straw for President Eisenhower.[4]

He knew Faubus couldn't be trusted to protect us and that it was time to act swiftly.

In an address September 24, 1957, Eisenhower said, "Mob rule cannot be allowed to override the decisions of our courts."

He intended to carry out court-mandated school desegregation and secure the Nine's safety.

From the Oval Office, Eisenhower referred to Arkansas leadership as "demagogic extremists".

He stated the Executive Branch was acting to enforce the decision of the federal courts.

His explained that his actions were necessary because courts orders were being ignored.

A former 5-Star Army General, he sent in the 101st Airborne Division to ensure the law was enforced.

President Eisenhower sent troops to Arkansas pursuant to law,

And "solely for the purposes of preventing interference with the orders of the court".

As President, he was Commander-In-Chief of all Armed Forces,

He was determined that we would make it into school either by will or by force.

On September 25, 1957, 101st Airborne soldiers protected us in a way no one else could,

They were fearless, strong, and prepared for anything the mob might try.

As we headed to school, it felt like we were headed to war.

Helicopters flew overhead and armed soldiers once again surrounded Central High.

More than 1,200 soldiers came to Little Rock to protect us.

But after the first day, soldiers of color were directed to stay at Camp Robinson's base.

The Arkansas National Guard was segregated and had no black soldiers at that time.

To minimize conflict, leaders ensured those carrying weapons were the crowd's same race.

The 101st Airborne Soldiers deployed from Fort Campbell, Kentucky, by plane.

They were decorated warfighters who took the mission of protecting us seriously.

They guarded the perimeter of Central High with bayonets affixed.

They were authorized to deal with protestors forcefully.

The 101st Airborne fought in a ferocious battle, "Operation Overlord" during World War II,

They were "Airborne," and "Air Assault," meaning they jumped to their fights from the sky.

They also served in Normandy during the Battle of the Bulge.

The soldiers were very professional in their duties, so we felt safe, and everyone knew why.

Incredibly, some segregationists tried to fight the 101st!

One man who wouldn't get out of the way received bayonet cuts.

By and large, most of the protestors eventually followed the soldiers' commands.

But two men who didn't comply were beaten with rifle butts.

For three days, Airborne soldiers escorted us to school in a station wagon.

In front and behind us were soldiers in gun-mounted military Jeeps.

When the convoy arrived at Central, more soldiers quickly surrounded us.

Unlike our last two attempts, we were well-protected with hearts so full we could leap!

As the soldiers led us up the steps to school,

I thought our torment was finally an issue of the past.

I felt proud while being escorted by fierce soldiers.

I hoped the main conflict was over, but our need for safekeeping would last.

We were sent to Principal Jess W. Matthews' office and assigned a soldier supposedly for our security.

Principal Matthews re-emphasized we could not fight, react, or respond if provoked.

If there was trouble, we were told to submit written reports to Vice Principal Elizabeth Huckaby,

But we soon realized the futility because our statements were ignored – it wasn't worth the pen stroke.

Authorities at Central collected many weapons brought to the school campus.

There were guns, knives, and ropes taken from racists with violent plans.

There would have been no way for us to protect ourselves from their attack,

But since the 101st was a Light Infantry Unit, they feared no man.

No matter what, the Nine knew nonviolence was the only choice.

If struck, we were told we couldn't fight back...we had to always turn the other cheek.

We knew we'd be watched extensively by school administrators – we couldn't even raise our voice.

We were expected to use nonviolent methods and, like Gandhi, be the change we seek.

Some student attackers were sent to the Principal's office for their actions.

He would simply give them a talking to and send them back to class.

Although there were at least 100 students who were expelled for violence against us that year,

The limited consequences for attacks against us were the reasons that they continued to last.

Of Central's 1,900 students, I believe less than 200 tried to physically hurt us throughout the year.

The indifference of the other students showed the fear of some, but other's apathy.

Some simply did not care as evidenced by turning their heads to avoid witnessing our attacks,

Their actions hurt far worse than our assailants and were much more impactive to me.

There was a prevailing mindset that African Americans should be glad for whatever they received.

Basically, we should be happy to attend Central High because we weren't worthy.

Although the Supreme Court's ruling did not imply school integration should come with strings,

School administrators continued to act like segregationists and extend our misery.

The 101st protected us in Little Rock for an entire month,

But they had to return to their base at Fort Campbell eventually.

President Eisenhower federalized the Army National Guard to revoke the governor's control.

By then, Governor Faubus was under investigation for his race-baiting tactics that were inflammatory.

We were incredibly sad to lose our 101st protective guardians.

It was very hard to return to school without the security of their defensive shield.

I was terrified because I never knew what would happen when they were gone.

If I wasn't being hit, I was being spat on or called horrible things...the hatred would never yield.

The Arkansas National Guard Soldiers weren't much older than we were.

They were lackadaisical in their duties, so our former security was now past.

The soldiers spent most of their time flirting with and chasing girls while on campus.

Their only duty was in the hallway; soldiers weren't allowed inside to protect us during class.

I tried to remain focused on doing well in school despite being bullied every day,

All nine of us learned to move quickly through the hallways to avoid human connection.

I was scared every day and prayed constantly.

We kept to ourselves and remained focused on our desire to achieve school integration.

Most of the teachers and administrators simply did not care.

If they didn't see an attack with their own eyes, they assumed it wasn't true.

Just like the segregationist protestors, they didn't want us there.

Although unfair, we were warned this was what the school leaders might do.

Sometimes I would stick straight pins on my book edges to prevent being grabbed.

I always held my books in front to shield my chest.

There were few consequences for their behavior, so our tormenters grew bold.

Although most didn't care if they were identified, attacks from behind were the greatest threat.

Bullies demanded, "Go back where you came from!" as if we weren't all from the same city.

They made demeaning songs out of racist phrases and sang them behind our backs in the hallway.

We made it a habit to NEVER sit down without first checking our seats for metal tacks.

We routinely endured items being thrown at us and being burned by cigarettes like human ash trays.

ARTIST STATEMENT
NANCY WILSON

Several years ago, my students and I were watching a grainy film clip of Elizabeth Eckford walking down Park Street encircled by a taunting mob. I was behind my students, looking over their heads at the film. I had seen the many photos and film clips before but having young people in front of me, who were Elizabeth's age, finally made the story more personal. I cried. Not just for her, but from a personal memory of trying so hard to just be accepted, and instead being taunted and threatened with a knife.

I was different. I walked with a limp caused by polio. Nothing of my experiences could compare with what Elizabeth faced that day and for the rest of the school year. But in a way, I understood.

Elizabeth's family member had sewn a special dress for her first day at school. She and her mother spent the rest of that day washing the spit from that lovingly made dress. Americans who spit on that dress and might have just as well have spit on the flag and the constitution. Elizabeth Eckford was only trying to receive a better education, a right guaranteed to all American citizens.

Being pushed down the steps was a huge threat since Central had them in abundant supply.

We also had to be careful to watch out for being scalded in the showers after PE.

Although difficult, we tried to maintain our sense of humor to lessen the sting of our pain.

I know I could not have endured what we suffered without the other eight who survived with me.

Parents even led afterschool meetings to coordinate the next day's attacks.

It was like a twisted school club established to raise future racists and promote bigotry.

Adults assigned roles to ensure that the Nine were attacked physically and mentally.

They also brought flyers for distribution to promote mindsets that were discriminatory.

The plans included everything from fights to dumping garbage on our backpacks,

One student was so vile that he urinated into the locker of Ernest Green.

Students threw metal objects that hurt, like locks and can openers.

They were the most well-planned and coordinated group of racists that I have ever seen!

Our lockers were routinely vandalized and our personal property destroyed.

Each time, the school simply replaced our school materials and sent us back to class.

At that time, parents had to buy their children's educational materials for school.

Had they been forced to pay for all those books, our family finances would not last!

So many things happened to us as while at Central.

I am just grateful that we survived the constant threats that took place.

We were physically and mentally abused repeatedly.

Our assailants tried to maintain the status quo and keep Central High one race.

One day, I was bullied to my wits' end and couldn't take it anymore.

I called my Grandfather and asked him to come get me from school.

He was the only man I knew that spoke to white people honestly and without fear.

Grandpa stood up for me, questioning the Principal's authority and his inability control or rule.

No. 176 *pam*

Office of the Deputy Chief of Staff for Military Operations

SITUATION REPORT: ARKANSAS
161700 - 171700 Eastern Standard Time December 1957

1. Summary of Events

    a. Minnie Brown, a Negro student, was suspended from Central High School for three days by Mr. Mathews, the school principal, for having spilled some food on two or three white students during the lunch period on 17 December 1957. Mr. Mathews has released the incident to the press.

    b. Central High School opened at 0830 hours, Central Standard Time, and closed at 1530 hours, Central Standard Time. Nine Negro students arrived and departed in private vehicles.

    c. There was no significant change in attendance at Central High School.

2. Dispositions

    a. Central High School

        One Platoon, 1st Battalion, 153d Infantry (Reinforced)

    b. Camp Robinson

        One Platoon, 1st Battalion, 153d Infantry (Reinforced) (30 minute alert)
        One Company, 1st Battalion, 153d Infantry (Reinforced) (1 hour alert)
        Balance of 1st Battalion, 153d Infantry (Reinforced)

Although I left, I only took the day's reprieve and returned to Central the very next day.

I simply could not let down the rest of the Nine and the other students counting on our victory.

Although I spent every day in fear, I had a sense of purpose and knew our effort was honorable.

I returned determined to see this effort to the end; if they wanted me out, they'd have to expel me.

Expulsion was a constant threat because we knew we were never wanted at Central.

It was clear there would be little leniency if we ever sought justice independently.

In November, Minnijean Brown spilled chili on a boy after tripping on a chair kicked in her way.

The cafeteria erupted in cheers from the cafeteria staff who witnessed our assaults daily.

Regardless of the circumstances, Minnijean was suspended from school for six days.

I envied her fearlessness and bravado despite the larger target placed on her back by our foes.

Minnijean was expelled as a "troublemaker" after fielding multiple attacks in February of 1958.

Afterward, Sammie Dean gleefully handed out flyers and buttons stating, "One down, eight to go."

Sammie Dean remained a key instigator at Central.
She controlled her classmates like a master puppeteer daily.
Although suspended for her segregationist actions and distribution of segregationist propaganda,
Due to public outcry and threats of a lawsuit, she unfortunately returned to continue her brutality.

With bullies like Sammie Dean and the others who physically assaulted us at school,
Every day we had to fight to maintain our composure and simply make it through.
I considered Thelma Mothershed to be my closest friend and a significant reason I remained,
If she could endure the toxic environment despite a heart murmur and medical challenges, I could too.

There were a few white students who were kind to me and other members of the Nine.
But they were considered "race traitors" by fellow classmates, abused and treated unfairly.
Two people made all the difference in the world to me during speech, my last class of the day.
They were Kendall Reinhard and Ann Williams. They saved my life, literally.

78

There were many unfortunate consequences for the few brave allies who showed the Nine kindness.

Thankfully, they did not give in to peer pressure despite horrific threats one could not conceive.

One household had to hire round-the-clock security, while other parents lost their jobs or businesses.

Their moral compass compelled them to do what was right although some families were forced to leave.

During our year at Central, the Little Rock Nine became the most famous teens in the world.

Our photographs were frequently featured in newspapers and international magazines.

We traveled to the White House and were interviewed constantly.

Some may have envied our fame, but we would have given it up to attend school in peace!

The Little Rock Nine were constantly surrounded by cameras,

Interviewers always wanted to know what we thought or did.

I understood the significance of our attempts to desegregate Central High were trying to do,

But since I was extremely quiet and shy, I considered this to be no way to live.

At the end of the year, officials didn't want Ernest Green to attend his graduation ceremonies.

They tried to discount his achievement by offering to mail his degree.

Having lost so much, Ernest refused to stay home and sacrifice one more thing.

His graduation was attended by Dr. Martin Luther King, Jr. and more than 125 soldiers and police.

We were all extremely proud of Ernest's accomplishment.

I was also grateful that we were able to make it through.

We survived despite the non-stop effort to have us removed.

But there was no rest; there was still much more fighting to do.

Ernest Green proudly participates in his graduation ceremony.

Governor Faubus sided with segregation again by shutting down every public high school in Little Rock,

He lied by blaming the federal government for his actions without shedding a tear.

He wasn't alone. Several counties nationwide opened private schools rather than integrate.

Some schools in Virginia and Maryland were closed for as many as seven years!

At school's end, forty-four teachers and administrators were fired from their posts.

Anyone considered a "desegregation sympathizer" was removed while segregationists laughed.

It did not matter that most of those fired had no connection to Central at all,

Clearly, administrators wanted to not only control the race of students, but also the mindset of staff.

Although teachers and administrators of both races lost their jobs,

Integration harmed African American teachers at a greater rate.

After desegregation, many white parents didn't want black teachers influencing their children,

Resulting in the loss of black teacher jobs despite their education or experience due to racial hate.

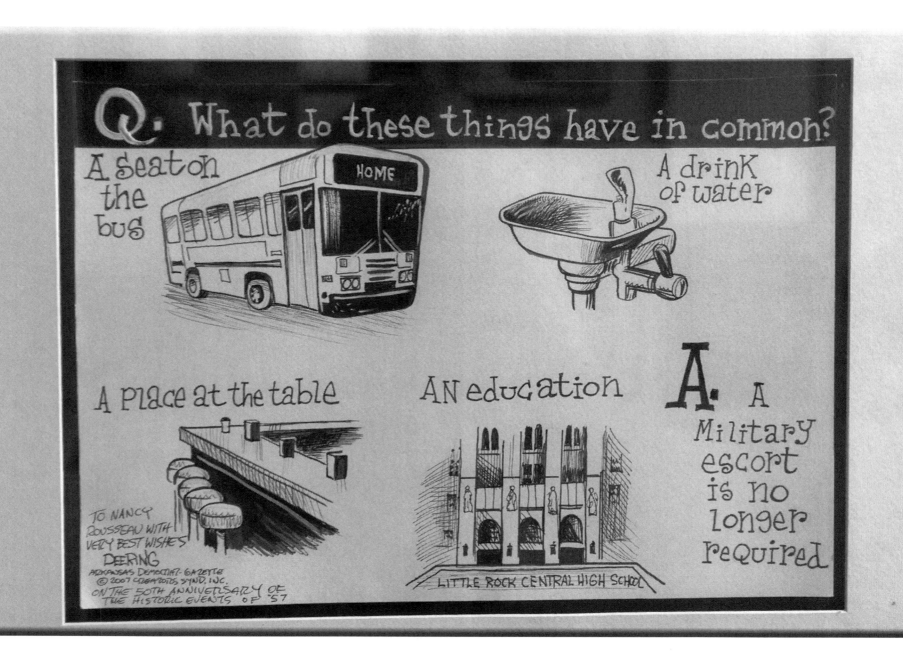

Our bodyguards were finally released, but federalizing the Guard came at a high price.
We were told more than two million dollars were spent for their lackluster protection.
I thought of so many ways that money could have been better spent,
Such as finishing Dunbar High or upgrading black students' education.

By the end of our school year, the Little Rock School Board had had enough.
They wanted to go back to their segregationist ways.
Although the Supreme Court Justices in Brown v. Board said desegregate "with all Deliberate Speed,"
The School Board continued to push back and delay.

Committees were formed on both sides of the desegregation issue during the lost year.
STOP (Stop This Outrageous Purge) protested the teachers' firings.
While CROSS (Committee to Retain Our Segregated Schools) sought to maintain the status quo.
Like most issues in Little Rock, the city was as divided and steeped in controversy.

"We the people" did not include everyone

When the founding fathers used this phrase in 1787, they did not have in mind the majority of America's citizens.

Justice Thurgood Marshall, 1987

The Aaron v. Cooper case advanced to the Supreme Court in September.

After initial arguments, the decision was made most expeditiously.

Despite segregationists' protests, the original Brown decision was upheld.

The states couldn't determine which decisions they would follow intermittently.

More than half of our Little Rock Nine families had to move after the school year.

Our parents were fired in retaliation for our efforts to desegregate.

Some fought back by making public the threatened loss of their jobs.

There were few middle-class employment options available so they left in haste.

My Mother lost her job at the Arkansas School for the Negro, Deaf and Blind.

It was painful because her job allowed her to watch my brother simultaneously.

He attended the school because he was developmentally delayed and autistic.

Although the loss was very hurtful, my Mom found another service job eventually.

About 3,600 students were impacted when Little Rock high schools closed.

Yet teachers were still expected to fulfil their contracts and sat in empty classrooms under Faubus' rule.

Families had to find alternative education for their children, either locally or out of town.

Some white students had private options, but few black students learned without public school.

A few churches offered tutoring classes to white students.

Some white students went straight to college when schools closed.

The end of formal education forced many to head straight to employment,

Since Faubus' decision impacted both whites and blacks, now the issue hit parents square on the nose.

During the "Lost Year", battles continued to prevent school integration.

There were fights, bombings, gassings, and violence in the streets.

During the last major segregation rally August of 1959, 250 protestors marched.

They paraded with Confederate flags and posters demanding schools remain closed to minorities.

During the protest, more than 20 arrests were made due to the mob's erratic behavior.

The fire department was called in to hose down protestors who were unruly.

Despite their racist, agitated screams, there was simply no avoiding future progress.

Like it or not, integration would soon become a reality.

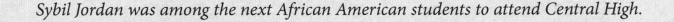

Sybil Jordan was among the next African American students to attend Central High.

While the School Board debated student placements,

Two white women threw gas canisters into the building scaring everyone alive.

Despite the meeting being forced to close with everyone making a mad dash to the exits,

No effort would prevent the eventuality of black students being assigned to Central in the fall of 1959.

Five courageous African American students were the next to attend Central High.

Carlotta and Jefferson were the only members of the original Nine to return, and they thrived.

The new students were Sybil Jordan, Sandra Johnson, and Franklin Henderson.

Instead of physical attacks, the new students were shunned between whispers as if they weren't alive.

For years, I internalized my feelings from the torment endured at Central High.

I didn't speak about what happened for almost forty years as I struggled through internal duress.

That changed in 1996 when I reunited with Ken and Ann, the only students who were compassionate to me.

I was grateful for the opportunity to tell them they saved my life through kindness.

I began speaking because I wanted people to understand the difference they could make.

Based on what I went through, I wanted to encourage anyone being tormented by bullying..

I hoped to inspire and encourage youth to mirror the support Kendall and Ann provided me,

A kind word can make a difference when one is attacked verbally, physically, or mentally.

The most persistent question I've received is, "Why did you stay at Central High?"

The Nine endured those horrific conditions because we understood the potential cost.

The future diversity of America's schools relied on our resilience and persistence,

If we did not remain, institutionalizing school desegregation could potentially be lost.

I attended Central because it offered the best education possible.

However, I never expected to pay so dearly for the instruction received!

Although my parents weren't formally educated, my family encouraged our academic excellence.

Grandfather routinely said, "Elizabeth, WHEN you go to college…" to me.

I knew my parents couldn't afford to send both myself and my sister to college.

They already struggled just to make ends meet and keep food on our plates.

Scholarships would be mandatory for us to enter a university.

Central High students received more scholarships than any other high school in the state.

After high school, I wanted to see the world and get out of Little Rock.

I eventually took a test in another county to certify my high school equivalency.

I attended Knox College on scholarship, but soon realized that it wasn't for me.

I thought, "What better way to see the world than to join the Army?"

I traveled with the Army to many bases throughout the States.

My first job was as a Pay Clerk, but I didn't like accounting.

Next, I served as an Information Specialist serving as a reporter for several bases.

But since I didn't initially know how to type, the job was time consuming and challenging!

Even military service didn't help me escape from issues of discrimination and segregation.

Throughout the late 60's and early 70's, race riots took place on installations internationally.

In 1971, I reported on a race riot on Fort McClellan, Alabama where I served.

With more than 2,000 members, the base held the world's largest number of the Women's Army Corps (WAC).

The riot was initiated after five black WACs were run down by a white driver.

He was caught and beaten, and a large protest ensued against disparate treatment and inequality.

More than 140 protesters were arrested, and I was sent to gather information for my Colonel,

It seemed wherever I went, violent racial issues continued to haunt me!

Many in the African American community were taking a stand against racial inequality,

Sparking a newfound sense of black power and pride.

The fight for equality was not new, it dated back to slavery.

The united effort within the Civil Rights Movement took the struggle to new heights.

The Civil Rights Act of 1964 provided much-needed federal protections.

The Act outlawed discrimination based on race, color, religion, sex, or national origin.

It rescinded laws upholding segregation and afforded equal safeguards to ALL.

The act was signed into law by President Lyndon B. Johnson.

President Lyndon B. Johnson was quoted as saying, "There are no problems we cannot solve together, and very few that we can solve by ourselves." on the occasion of signing the Civil Rights Act in 1964.

I am proud to have served as a youth in the battle for equal rights for all citizens.

But many civil rights warriors paid a much higher price for seeking rights that would no longer wait.

In 1963, the Ku Klux Klan bombed a church in Birmingham, killing four little girls to protest school desegregation,

And a racist assassin's bullet shot and killed Dr. Martin Luther King, Jr. in 1968.

After leaving the military, I held several jobs and became a bit of a rolling stone.

I returned to Little Rock because I realized there was simply no place like home.

For many years, I wrestled with past demons before serving as a probation officer for a county judge.

It was healing to be with my family in a safe environment where I was loved and known.

Although some still supported segregation,

The overall mindset in Little Rock changed gradually.

Instead of being a source of embarrassment,

The Little Rock Nine became celebrated within the city!

Congressional Gold Medal in honor of the four 16th Street Bombing victims.

In 1987, events started being held to recognize the contributions of the Little Rock Nine.

Held every ten years, the recognitions have exponentially grown.

The first was held at the Arkansas State Capitol by former Governor William J. Clinton.

While we were at Central, he was an 11-year old living in Hope, Arkansas; to him, our story was known.

Ten years later marked the first city-wide celebration commemorating our 40th anniversary.

For that event, Will Counts coordinated a photo shoot for Hazel Massery and me.[5]

Although Hazel apologized via phone in 1963, I hadn't seen her since the infamous attack.

Her parents transferred her from Central when they knew the school would reflect diversity.

Hazel was still living in Little Rock with her high school sweetheart as a wife and mother.[6]

Counts called our photo, "Reconciliation" and we gave speeches together promoting racial harmony.

But audience members would often attack Hazel during our talks for her actions as a teen,

Our interactions became strained because I didn't feel she acknowledged what happened sincerely.

Regarding our famous photo, Hazel would remark, "Life is more than one moment."
Yet she would not acknowledge several post-attack interviews where she continued to use racial slurs.
I truly believe we must honestly acknowledge our painful but shared past to achieve reconciliation.
Empathy is inauthentic without true acknowledgement of one's own actions and words.

I tell my story to initiate and encourage real conversations within the next generation.
Open communication is the only way to achieve understanding and racial peace.
Transparent communications are critical; however
Without honesty and sincerity no effort will matter in the least.

The Little Rock Nine 50th Anniversary celebration was our largest event yet.[7]

We were reunited with our beloved 101st Airborne Soldiers who dedicatedly protected us.

Everywhere we turned, there was a sea of supporters, politicians, celebrities, and dignitaries.

That included our fellow young civil rights activist turned Congressman, Representative John Lewis.

Former President and Arkansas Governor William J. Clinton officiated our 50th ceremony.

Afterward, he held open doors once barred from our entry.

Two years later, President Clinton awarded the Little Rock Nine the Congressional Gold Medal.

Voted by members Congress, it is the highest award given to American civilians.

During the 50th celebration, the Little Rock Central High National Park Service was dedicated.
It chronicles in detail what we endured throughout the Central High Crisis for all the world to see.
Each year, more than 150,000 visitors tour the facility and our old high school across the street.
Now, our contributions to the Civil Rights Movement are displayed for posterity.

In 2008, I saw something I never imagined.
President Barack H. Obama was elected as the first African American President of the country.
The Little Rock Nine were invited by the Arkansas Congressional Delegation to attend his inauguration,
But I still had difficulty in large groups and did not want to be caught in an unbearable, massive crowd.

2017 marks the 60th year of our post-Central High journey.

As we age, our focus turns to the future of our legacy.

Supporters can join us by reporting bullies, fighting oppression and standing for justice and unity,

Our sacrifices are appreciated when we see students take full advantage of today's opportunities!

I returned to Central High to share my experiences and commemorate the 60th anniversary.

It was an honor to speak to future leaders who wanted to elevate their understanding and knowledge higher.

It was truly rewarding to be so warmly received by the students,

A complete reversal from what I endured more than half a century prior.

I continue to present to audiences in the hope of helping them understand.

We have great a responsibility to one another as fellow residents of the world.

Please, be caring and compassionate to one another,

Don't be known as the source of violence or the place from where offensive language is hurled.

This year, we commemorated another event I never thought I would see,
The Little Rock Nine spoke at the first Smithsonian museum dedicated solely to African American history!
I was initially excited to see the exhibits at the National Museum of African American History and Culture,
But after seeing several displays, I felt overwhelmed and compelled to leave.

Although 60 years have passed, my encounters at Central High remain with me in many ways.
It is very difficult for me to view racial oppression or hostility without being impacted viscerally.
To this day, I avoid large crowds and loud noises at all costs.
After speaking engagements, my audiences "clap" by waving their hands out of respect for me.

I take great pride in the accomplishments the Little Rock Nine achieved.
Looking back, I sincerely regret the high price paid by our friends and families.
Although challenges remain, I know our loved ones would be truly astonished by today's advances.
Despite their sacrifices, I believe they would consider our effort to desegregate Central to be worthy.

HEADQUARTERS

ARKANSAS NATIONAL GUARD

CAMP ROBINSON ARKANSAS

COMMAND REPORT

OPERATION ARKANSAS

My junior year of high school was more of a military operation than an education,

Complete with safeguard from the best warfighters available in America's Army.

It set the tone for future battles yet to be waged.

Civil Rights leaders fought for equal opportunity and rights for all of humanity.

Know that bullies are influenced by what they were taught and their own personal insecurities.

When they lash out against your uniqueness, they expose their own self-doubts in a distorted way.

I know what it is to endure the endless taunts of tormentors and persons filled with hate,

But hurting myself or suicide due to someone else's shortcomings was never an option –
   give tomorrow one more day!

COMMEMORATING 60 YEARS

Many students tell me they could never do what the Little Rock Nine did.

When serving the greater good, you never know what you can do until you try.

Most of the Civil Rights Movement was accomplished by ordinary people.

Trust yourself. Deep inside, you have the capability to face any challenge that comes by.

My dream for tomorrow is that we never return to yesteryear.

Though we've made much progress toward equity for all, unfortunately we seem to be beginning to digress.

I implore you to protect one another, speak truth, and walk with integrity.

You are the key to achieving a future that embraces unity, civility, respect and kindness.

I am humbled each time I speak to the talented, brilliant, and fearless youth of today.
You are champions of justice and equity and give me great hope for the future world you will soon lead.
Please take full advantage of your education to develop and prepare you.
You have the potential to help our global community and most surely you will succeed.

Remember my first day at Central the next time you're
    having a bad day at work or at school.
It proves there is no limit to what you can achieve despite
    naysayers who attack and berate.
Know that I am extremely proud of you and always want you
    to confidently with your head held high.
Most importantly, when faced with adversity, follow my
    lead and #WalkPastHate!

#WalkPastHate

Epilogue
Central High Today

Nancy Rousseau
Principal, Central High

Nine brave black students, mere teenagers aged 14-17, changed the world forever. I have been honored to work with the members of the Little Rock Nine for more than 20 years. The City of Little Rock hosted its first city-wide recognition on the 40th Anniversary of the desegregation of Central High in 1997. At the time, I was Assistant Principal at Central High. By the 50th Anniversary, I had become Principal, and I proudly continue to support as co-chairperson of the entire event.

September 20, 2017, Central High students were treated to a special presentation by Elizabeth Eckford, the first member of the Little Rock Nine to arrive at Central High and Dr. Eurydice Stanley to kick off our school 60th Anniversary celebration. Having known Elizabeth for more than 20 years, I was so proud of her and so proud for her as she shared a preview of this book with Central students. Her confidence and ease in speaking was in complete contrast to presentations in years past where she became overwhelmed by the memories of what happened to her at Central High. It was so encouraging to see her speaking with poise and confidence as she shared important history with our students, the backstory of the Central High Crisis and the perfect storm that led to the need for 101st Airborne soldiers to protect her and the Little Rock Nine while on campus all those years ago.

Sixty years later, Central High is a completely different school. Diversity is our backbone, and it is celebrated here daily. There are currently 27 languages spoken by families that attend Central, representing 24 countries.

While it is not a perfect world, the Central High School of today wears a very different face from that in 1957.

Central High School remains at the center of academic excellence in Little Rock and the State of Arkansas. We are consistently at the forefront with our National Merit Semifinalists, our Advanced Placement Scholars, and our students' scholarships. Additionally, 35 advanced placement classes allow our students to take college courses. We have a program to meet the needs of every entering freshmen.

Central High School is the only high school with the distinction of being a National Park Service Historic Site. Our students routinely take field trips across the street to the Little Rock Central High School National Historic Site to learn about the heroic pioneers who integrated their school. More than 125,000 visitors tour the park annually, including a tour of Central High. Every student at Central connects with our school's history.

There is indeed a special magic at Central High school that exists due to our controversial history, the beautiful architecture of our building and our long legacy of academic excellence. We all recognize that the events of 1957 changed the face of our school forever.

The courage and perseverance of the Little Rock Nine and their quest for an equitable education serves as a model for our students in 2017 and beyond.

Just Like Elizabeth

By Paige Mitchell
11th Grader, Central High

We all can say that we have had times
when we had to confront our demons
or simply just put up a little more effort,
which simply reminds me of Elizabeth Eckford.

Her first day at Central she rode the bus alone,
she didn't know to ride with everyone else
because she didn't have a phone.
People hit her,
they spit on her,
and called her everything but what she was,
which was courageous.

And there was a time when people bullied me,
and called me names so I had to be courageous.
I was 12 years old, and I had no clue
that people judged me just by my shoes.
I had no clue that I couldn't be true
to myself if I wanted to fit in.

But I had a best friend,
and a picture frame family,
even though I was the black sheep
and I cried myself to sleep.
I just sat down and cried, like Elizabeth did on that bus the first day,
in that brand-new dress that she and her sister made.

I guess even 60 years ago
peers cared about your clothes just the same.
But it all changed for her in a matter of a few weeks
and it was just the same for me.

I had a lot of bad in store.
I noticed my mama wasn't wearing her ring no more,
and my best friend called and said we weren't friends no more,
and kids at school laughed and said I dressed like I was poor.

Just like Elizabeth,
I was afraid to go to school.
Every single day was another bad day, and another sad day,
but I'm not a sad person,
so I looked the other way.

Just like Elizabeth
I had to put on a brave face.
So people couldn't know how tough I was hurting inside.
So people couldn't know how much I cried.

Just like Elizabeth,
There was a time when I was purely devastated.
But would you look at me now? I am surely celebrating all the blessings that
have fallen on my lap!
Just like her I went and took my happiness right back!

And my mom's figuring out how to be a single parent with four kids,
That friend that left me behind, we figured out how to be sisters again.
The school Elizabeth couldn't go to at first, I strut right in,
and everybody calls me "ranch" 'cause I be dressing!

Nine students changed it all by just going to school,
and I'm hoping one day that I can change the world too.

Thank you, Elizabeth Eckford.

Reflections of Progress and Healing
Robin White
Superintendent, Little Rock Central High National Park Service

Sixty years ago, nine African American students faced domestic terrorism while pursuing equal education. In the fall of 1957, Little Rock, Arkansas became the national symbol of change. The integration of Central High School would become a landmark battle in the struggle for civil rights. While conflict between the state and federal government played out in public, the real battle continued in the classroom and the corridors of the school. Physical and psychological warfare weighed on the shoulders of nine young students who served as ambassadors of moral courage.

The Little Rock Central High School National Historic Site was approved November 6, 1998 and dedicated during the 50th Anniversary of the desegregation of Central High September 25, 2007. The facility is a 1,717-square-foot facility that hosts our Central High Crisis exhibit, auditorium, bookstore, additional collections, and administrative offices.

The park receives 125,000 to 150,000 visitors on average every year from vast and varied international backgrounds. We provide multiple programs that range from Junior Rangers to informal tours. Our facility also hosts performing arts demonstrations, trainings, and civil rights workshops in partnership with organizations such as the Little Rock School District, higher learning institutions, the City of Little Rock, and youth organizations.

We hold numerous events throughout the year, most recently a viewing of the film Marshall which told the narrative of Supreme Court Justice Thurgood Marshall in support of the Central High integration 60th anniversary. Marshall fought against the ideology of second class citizenship based on race while valuing the concept of humanity. This powerful film showcases his efforts to promote equality. It comes at a time when we are once again faced with the degradation of a people. This film reinforces why it is vital to value our differences, and reinforces why individuals such as Thurgood Marshall, Leonard Peltier, Jack Greenburg, Constance Baker, Daisy and L.C. Bates, Charles Hamilton Houston and other intellectual giants fought against racism and discrimination.

America's National Park Service can be aptly described as America's Crown Jewel. They coordinate majestic sites designed for recreation, relaxation, and reflection. Our Little Rock site provides common ground to provoke shared dialogue for public awareness of our nation's transformative struggle towards equality.

We provide a forum for visitors to share their narratives. As of late, we have also become a sanctuary for healing, with circle talks regarding race and conflict. We are standing at the crossroads of a social movement. It is challenging to be optimistic when faced with recent events such as the Charleston Nine Massacre and the unwarranted rage in Charlottesville, Virginia. Heather Heyer is a 21st Century Viola Liuzzo. Collectively, we can only strive for a greater consciousness.

I encourage you to be a place of inspiration and hope, and to celebrate that which binds, not divides us. The strength of the Little Rock Nine is demonstrated by the power of their self-governance. Their spirit could not be contained on the road to social justice. We are all beneficiaries of the Little Rock Nine, along with other leaders such as Thurgood Marshall, Sanford Tollette, Dr. Sybil Hampton, and Lottie Shackleford. They remain symbolic beacons of hope. Their legacies show that it is good to fight for a specific purpose, and even better to fight on purpose.

When we walk in pursuance of healing and hope, we move beyond our bankrupt status by facilitating major conscience and engagement by connecting with our historical memory. Together, we have the capacity to address social oppression and legislated racism, addressing the legacy of America's untreated trauma. By doing so, we will be able to move beyond our fears.

May you find your special niche to walk in grace and beauty.

A Call to Action: The Cost of Silence
For Parents, Teachers, and Leaders
Dr. Eurydice Stanley, LTC (Retired)

In 1957, people around the world were introduced to Elizabeth Eckford through a photograph. The image bore witness to her character and her persecution while attempting to do something so seemingly egregious as seeking the best education possible. The image shamed and shocked the nation, placing a face on racism.

Leaders, teachers, parents, and adults, if an image were taken behind the scenes of your organization or home, what would it capture? The 1957 Little Rock Central High Crisis is a call to action to recognize the cost of silence and the importance of not becoming complacent. Silence can imply agreement. If inclusion is your goal, ensure your message is loud and clear.

Hate, prejudice, and acts of discrimination flourish in environments where the only action by bystanders is to look the other way. As evidenced by the primary characters in this book, your voice and behaviors matter. Tomorrow's leaders are relying upon you to engage when misconduct is observed.

As teens, the Little Rock Nine fought a courageous battle in a volatile setting made more debilitating by the lack of school and community leader intervention. Although the Nine's attacks were reported, they were ignored. Although their voices were silenced, their presence could not be denied.

The 1957 Little Rock Central High Crisis serves as an excellent case study for leaders. With this book, Elizabeth hopes to inspire people of all ages to be courageous while facing trials. Additionally, she hopes to also remind leaders of the opportunity cost of not protecting personnel under their charge.

President Eisenhower refused to maintain the status quo and look the other way while Governor Faubus advanced his political career by catering to segregationists. President Eisenhower gave Arkansas leadership ample time and opportunity to rectify the situation. When they didn't act, he engaged.

As a former five-star general and Supreme Allied Commander during World War II, Eisenhower was accustomed to making decisions. Alex Wilson's beating served as the final straw. What is your final straw? When that bridge is crossed, are you willing to "send in the troops" like President Eisenhower did with the 101st Airborne? Do your personnel clearly understand where you draw the line?

If your organizational culture has diverted from its stated vision and mission, extremes may be necessary for realignment. Eisenhower placed the safety of people and the need to maintain order first. His actions establish a critical standard for those in charge – gather data, analyze the facts, then act swiftly and decisively. He provides an exceptional blueprint for today's leaders.

I first met Elizabeth in 1999 while on temporary military assignment in Little Rock. I visited the former Little Rock Central High School Museum located in the historic Mobil service station across the street from the school before the national park service was founded. It was there that I saw Will Count's poster titled "Reconciliation." The images gave vision to my doctoral research on race and reconciliation in the Christian church and provided a blueprint for what I hoped to achieve.

The contrasting images were intriguing. In the lower corner was the famous black and white photo of Hazel Bryan Massery screaming behind Elizabeth as seen on page 32, her face contorted with hate. I was struck because as an African American woman, I have seen the same hateful facial distortion more times than I care to admit. Counts perfectly captured Hazel's rage and intolerance, balanced by Elizabeth's grace under pressure.

It is no wonder that the image became one of the most iconic photographs of the 20th century.

The poster's larger color image was of Elizabeth and Hazel standing arm in arm, smiling, as seen on page 100 of this book. THAT was the outcome I hoped to achieve through my research. The museum was sold out of posters at the time, but thankfully, they allowed me to purchase the last poster on display despite it being torn. The Park Ranger must have recognized my earnestness, because I was placed in contact with both women and they graciously granted interviews.

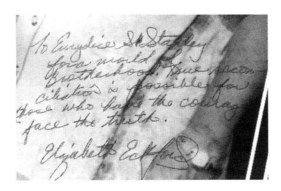

Although understandably guarded, Elizabeth and I connected during our interview and became friends. She is a remarkable woman who mentored me throughout the remainder of my military career, always sharing sage advice. I considered myself extremely lucky to be able to speak with her, and watched my own children become emboldened through the years by knowing and sharing "Auntie Elizabeth's" story.

Despite being subjected to a horrific ordeal her first day of school, Elizabeth maintained her dignity and showed the world the power of one person. I was always incredulous when Elizabeth did not consider what she did to be remarkable due to her constant fear. However, she was afraid yet remained. She remained laser focused on her goal and committed to the other members of the Little Rock Nine. Over the course of the year, the Nine displayed the power of a team. They relied upon one another and empathized with one another although each of their journeys were individualized while attending separate classes at Central.

Elizabeth gives a unique perspective to what was previously considered "a bad day". Anyone facing adversity are encouraged to follow her example and mantra, #WalkPastHate. After 60 years, Elizabeth is still standing and silent no more. She chooses to share her story to empower those being bullied or maltreated in schools, organizations, on social media or within their respective communities. Elizabeth knows the importance of her message having lived it personally.

Now that she has found her voice, she speaks to increase the confidence and mettle of others to help to find their own.

The issues the Little Rock Nine faced as teens belied their age. Their story inspires because they remained focused and shone like stars despite the incessant attempts of naysayers to undermine their success. The Nine reinforce the importance of resilience when pursuing one's goals and dreams.

Influencers promote organizational integrity and actively seek to create a culture that embraces and empowers team members. Encourage team members to follow the empathetic lead of Ann Williams and Kendall Reinhardt, Elizabeth's only friends at Central aside from the Nine. If members of the organization have become apathetic, similar bridgebuilders will be critical to reclaim them and bring dispirited personnel back into the fold.

Great leaders model desired behavior to establish an ideal organizational culture. Remember the global impact of Counts' photograph and remain cognizant of your organizational image. Routinely assess your organization. If improper behavior is identified, remember Elizabeth's ordeal and act decisively and courageously.

The opportunity cost of apathetic leadership is simply too great of a price to pay. By remaining vigilant and proactive, leaders ensure their organizational image remains a source of pride. Reflect your desired image and establish an organizational culture that demands and expects the full inclusion of every member of the team to ensure organizational success.

Stranger Danger

Grace Stanley
CEO, Missing Petals

One might wonder why Elizabeth didn't leave the bus stop bench with Mr. Bates or her fellow classmate when she had the chance. She notes that her Mother was very protective and even adamant about her not being alone with strangers. Obviously, Mrs. Eckford's messages to her daughter were very strong. Parents and caregivers, have you had a talk with your children to ensure they know your expectations regarding strangers?

Although Elizabeth's situation at Central High was horrible, it could have been even worse. Many stalkers take advantage of children by pretending to help them when they are most vulnerable. They gain their trust and then force them to perform acts that they do not want to do by threatening their life or their family and keeping them trapped.

Human Trafficking and child predators weren't discussed as frequently in the 1950's as they are today. The occurrences took place, even within families, but weren't discussed. Please ensure that you speak with your youth about good touches and bad touches and maintaining personal boundaries. Most importantly, encourage them to tell a parent, caregiver, or teacher when someone makes them feel uncomfortable.

The thing that I hope people recognize most is not that Elizabeth's Mother was "The Queen of No," but that she was with good reason. Mrs. Eckford was trying to protect her daughter in a racist, segregationist environment where few people cared about what happened to young black girls. That situation continues to impact us today.

I founded my Human Trafficking Awareness company, Missing Petals, after 300 girls were stolen from school in Nigeria. I had to Google Human Trafficking because I didn't know what it was. I was horrified by what I saw, and spent my time in the Young Entrepreneur Academy devoted to finding out a way to ensure this wouldn't happen to anyone else. The hashtag #BringBackOurGirls was everywhere, and I wanted the girls to be returned home like everyone else in the world.

I was 11 years old at the time, and although my Mom had spoken with me about good touches and bad touches ever since I was a little girl, I never hear about Human Trafficking before. I thought something like this would be shared in schools. Since it wasn't, I wanted to fill the void. I tell students that Human Trafficking is a global billion-dollar industry. Children as young as four years old have been stolen. Over 80% of people in sex trafficking are under the age of 18. And most importantly, no one is safe, regardless of their background, race, or age.

The Missing Petals logo is a sunflower with one quarter of its petals missing to represent the quarter of the population currently missing due to Human Trafficking. Children need to understand this very real danger. The one good thing that is apparent from Elizabeth Eckford's encounters at Central is she was well prepared by her Mom. Elizabeth knew to keep her wits about her while under pressure in that aggressive crowd. She also knew what her Mom's expectations were, and that her Mother loved her and wanted her to remain safe. Please follow Mrs. Eckford's lead by having that important discussion with the children you care about today!

When I speak to youth about the dangers of human trafficking, I encourage them never to run away from home. Children can think they are getting back at their caregivers by running away, but can instead be placing themselves in real danger. One-third of the teens that run away from home are lured into Human Trafficking within 48 hours, with only two percent of the victims ever escaping.

Please have this important talk with your children and make your guidance clear. Elizabeth knew what her Mother's expectations were – do your children? Send your youth to my website, www.missingpetals.com, for more safety tips and a "Missing Petals" bracelet to remind your children to remain aware of their surroundings.

For more Human Trafficking statistics, visit www.justice.gov/humantrafficking.

Acknowledgements

Many thanks to our family, friends and those who believed in us and supported us throughout this project. We would especially like to thank Dr. Jordan, Principal Rousseau, the Little Rock Central High National Park Service, the Arkansas National Guard Museum, Dr. David Ware, Capitol Historian, and Superintendent White for sharing their insights and resources with our readers. We know that this project would not be possible without the special talents of wonderful friends, to include: the mastery of our book designer, Thomas Cunningham; the captivating photography of Kirk Jordan; the watchful eye of our "word sleuth" and editor, JoAnne French; the incredible artwork of Rachel Gibson; the talented students of Central High, past and present; and the unwavering encouragement of Stella Cameron, Central High's incredible librarian.

Eurydice and Grace thank Grandma Bernice Rozell for loving us to the moon and back and Grandma Priscilla and Pa-Pa Stephens, Sr. for being our biggest cheerleaders!

Special thanks to Anna and Calvin for providing such beautiful family dinners that perfectly fueled our book discussions. You prove that southern hospitality is alive and well!

Most importantly, this book would not have been possible without the support of contributors who believed in our dream to help make it a reality. Thank you for supporting the vision of this project and recognizing the importance of Elizabeth's message. Your sponsorship has made this possible!

The Protectors
The Very Rev. Dr. and Mrs. Christoph Keller, III Dr. Sybil Hampton

The Allies
Nancy B. Moyle
LTC (Ret) Quewanncoii C. Stephens, Sr.
Jamie N. Goins Arreola, M.A.Ed.

The Flag Salute

The Advocates
Michael, Monica & Micaela Bailey
Tom Schecker
Jana Johnson Davis
Dr. Carolyn Greene
Amy Bell
Norris Sumrall
Martin S. Irons, Esquire
Ronald Olufunwa
Ranger Jodi Morris
Thomas Cunningham IV and Family
Naomi Baldwin

The Supporters
Sonya Jackson Myles
Landon & Anita Tucker
Jimmy & Dina Watts
Tamara Estrill-Lett
Dr. Jessica Bullard
C.O. Brown
Mark & Tiffany Harper
Dr. Mickey and Diane Dansby
Adam Seymore Kunz

James and Jessica Hampton
Lisa Harris
Tonja Matthews
Sharon Bliss
Patrice Brown
Brenda McCreary
Mykenzi Davis-Cowart
Jayna N. Lassiter
Dr. Laquita Blockson
The Gibson Family
Laura Frombach
Tara Rolstad
Twanna Lumpkins
Kiki Bryant
Quinton and Stephanie McCorvey
Daniel Marshall
Jennifer Johnson Clark
Maria Antoinette

The Helpers
Andrea Fernandes
Sarah Elizabeth Bradford

About the Contributors

$\mathcal{E}$LIZABETH ECKFORD was the first member of the Little Rock Nine to arrive at Central High. While only a teen, she bravely withstood being blocked from school by armed soldiers and faced an incensed, segregationist mob alone. Images of her attack showed the world the face of discrimination, to the embarrassment of the nation. International images of Elizabeth's attack sparked global outcry against racism and discrimination, resulting in President Dwight D. Eisenhower sending in the 101st Airborne for the students' safeguard.

The daughter of Birdie and Oscar Eckford, Elizabeth is one of six siblings. She attended Central for one year and was homeschooled after the public high schools were closed to prevent desegregation. Elizabeth attended Knox college before joining the Army as a member of the Women's Army Corps (WAC), serving five years. Her initial assignment was as a pay clerk before serving as an information specialist writing articles for newspapers at Fort Benjamin Harrison, Indiana, and Fort McClellan, Alabama. She was awarded the Army Good Conduct medal while on active duty.

After leaving the military, Elizabeth held a variety of positions prior to returning to Little Rock where she surrounded herself by family and raise her sons, Erin and Calvin. She achieved her goal of obtaining a college degree when she earned her BA in history from Central State University in Wilberforce, Ohio. She served as a Probation Officer for County Circuit Court Judge Marion Humphrey for ten years, retiring in 2009.

For her courageous acts as a member of the Little Rock Nine, Elizabeth received numerous awards from organizations grateful for their personal sacrifice and contributions to society. Most notably the Little Rock nine in 1999 received from President William J. Clinton the Congressional Gold Medal, our country's highest civilian award. The Little Rock Nine have been honored with a United States Postal Service stamp in 2005 and a commemorative one-dollar coin from the United States Mint issued in 2007. In 2010, the Little Rock Nine received the Pere Marquette Discovery Award, the university's highest honor for those who achieve an extraordinary breakthrough that adds to the advancement of human knowledge or the advancement of humanity.

In 2015 the Nine received the prestigious Lincoln Leadership Prize from the Abraham Lincoln Presidential Library Foundation for exceptional character, conscience, commitment to democracy and service. While teens, the Nine and Mrs. Bates received the Spingarn Medal from the National Association for the Advancement of Colored People (NAACP) in 1958 for upholding the basic ideals of American democracy and outstanding achievement. She shares with Hazel Bryan Massery the Father Joseph Blitz Award presented by the National Conference for Community and Justice. The Nine were inducted into the Arkansas Black Hall of Fame in 2007.

Elizabeth continues to reside in her beloved Little Rock and takes great delight in gardening and speaking with youth, who inspire her and continue her healing process. She resides in her childhood home with her sister, Anna Eckford Goynes, and son Calvin.

DR. EURYDICE STANLEY is an International Motivational Speaker, Author, retired Army Veteran, and full-time Mommy. She is founder of Amused Media and Productions, LLC, an organizational development company. Her educational sessions leverage nearly 28-years of experience providing training for members of every Department of Defense branch of service as a Senior Human Resources Manager, retiring as a Lieutenant Colonel in 2014. In the military, she specialized in presentations and developing research in the areas of leadership, diversity, inclusion, personality, and a wide range of human relations topics.

"Mom Who Serves" on HLN's Morning Express with Robin Meade.

After losing both of her dearly loved brothers, Quewanncoii C. Stephens, II and Aaron O. Weiss within a calendar year, Dr. Eurydice expanded efforts with her nonprofit, The Transition Foundation, Inc. to include Vet Honor Help Hope. The organization raises awareness for issues impacting the Veteran community, particularly suicide. They host events throughout the year as well as an annual international virtual walk on Veterans Day. She blogs on 50Revelations.com and manages several Facebook pages to include *Dr. Eurydice, Family CEO First* and *Stand United Against Racism.*

"Dr. Eurydice" has always been an avid writer. She has published more than 100 articles and authored three books, *God's Grace: Psalms of Love, Laughter, Tears and Praise from Mother to Daughter; God's Grace II: Pearls of Love and Encouragement for Princesses of All Ages* and *Lil' Man, All Boy: Christian MENtorship.* She is a John C. Maxwell Certified speaker, trainer and leadership consultant and served on his Presidential Advisory Council, specializing in youth. Students she worked with in the past received numerous awards for innovative community outreach and service. She holds numerous certifications in speech, training, leadership and instructional design with organizations such as Paradigm Personality Labs and the Sarasota Academy of Christian Counselors.

Eurydice's awards include the Army Distinguished Military Service Medal and distinguished service commendations from the state of Florida for her support of eight Gulf Coast hurricane operations in several key Florida National Guard positions. She received the Adjutant General's Corps Achievement Medal for supporting Wounded Warriors, was featured on the cover of Military Advanced Education for innovative strategies promoting Service Member education and was twice recognized as an exceptional

Born in Paso Robles, California, Eurydice developed a love for travel as an "Army Brat" and throughout her military career. In addition to studying International Business in Lyon, France, she is a legacy graduate of her beloved Florida A&M University, earning a BS in Public Management. A member of her family has attended FAMU since it was founded in 1887. She also attended University of Minnesota-Twin Cities, earning a Master of Arts in Industrial Relations; and Louisiana Baptist University, where sge received her PhD in Christian Counseling and Psychology.

Whenever she is not driving her daughter, Grace, and son, Christian, to their next adventures in the family minivan, Eurydice enjoys travelling. She is a proud Silver Star member of Alpha Kappa Alpha Sorority, Incorporated, and has life memberships with Florida A&M University and the Association of the United States Army (AUSA). Eurydice is a Distinguished Toastmaster with Toastmasters, International and is active in her community. She believes everyone has the responsibility to positively influence the next generation. She can be reached on her website, www.dreurydice.com.

GRACE STANLEY is a gifted 15-year-old freshman who attends West Florida High School where she majors in Biomedical Sciences. A member of the Jaguar Freshman Volleyball team, Grace was selected "Most Inspirational" by her coaches. She is also a member of the Drama Club, Key Club, and the International Thespian Society.

A budding historian, Grace has advanced to the Florida State Finals of National History Day for three years in a row. In 2017, she was reached the semi-finals for her documentary about the 6888th Central Postal Directory Battalion. She received the Florida State History Fair Day World War II award from the Florida State University Institute on World War II and the Human Experience. She is currently expanding her documentary about the 6888th with her mother.

Grace has received many prestigious awards despite her young age, including the White House Presidential Award of Merit from President Obama for academic excellence in 2014 and Region V NAACP Gloster P. Current Youth Leadership Award in 2015. She has also been recognized for exceptional writing in the essay competition of the Florida Commission on the Status of Women, placing second in 2016 and first in 2017. Grace was also a State Finalist in the State PTA "Reflections" poetry competition.

A budding entrepreneur, Grace is CEO of Missing Petals, a nonprofit

dedicated to raising human trafficking awareness "Until Every Child Comes Home". Her presentations outline safety strategies and awareness messages to keep youth safe. She founded Missing Petals in 2011 while participating in the Pensacola Young Entrepreneur Academy. She won third place overall for her business plan and was awarded the highest amount of donations from the "Shark Tank" investor panel.

Grace has benefitted extensively from the mentorship of extended FAMUly and by participating in programs such as the Mobley-Thompson Creativity and Innovation Summer Academy at the FAMU School of Business and Industry (2015), the Harvard University Mock Trial Association Debates serving on the Rusty and River Fields Foundation team (2016), the General Daniel "Chappie" James Summer Flight Academy (2016) and "Peace Jam", an international leadership program that allows students to be mentored by Nobel Peace Prize Laureates (2017).

Grace has earned two Taekwondo Black Belts from separate leagues and is a member of the St. John Divine Missionary Baptist Church children's choir. She enjoys reading, learning cultural dances, travelling, and spending time with friends and family. Already a "Rattler" at heart, Grace hopes to attend Florida A&M University as her first educational institution on the path to become an obstetrician in the future.

WILL COUNTS worked as a photographer for the Arkansas Democrat during the Central High Crisis between 1957 and 1960. His photographs were runner-up for the 1957 Pulitzer Prize in photography. He became a photo editor for the Associated Press in Chicago in 1960 and later an AP photographer in Indianapolis. He returned to Central forty years later to document changes to the school and created "Reconciliation" reuniting Elizabeth Eckford and Hazel Bryan Massery. He was a Professor Emeritus of the Indiana University School of Journalism prior to his death in 2001. His wife and children donated his photograph collection, including the Central High Crisis images to the Indiana University Archives. He is survived by his wife Vivian, a daughter Claudia and a son Wyatt.

RACHEL GIBSON is an illustrator/graphic designer from Longview, Texas. She is a graphic design student at Harding University. She created the artwork for the Civil Rights Memory Project at Little Rock Central High, sponsored by the Butler Center for Arkansas Studies at the Central Arkansas Library. She enjoys French Toast, and being outside. She is passionate about illustration and plans to continue to illustrate important messages wherever life takes her.

KIRK JORDAN - is chief photographer for the Department of Arkansas Parks and Tourism. He enjoys taking pictures of natural things in less conventional ways, and finding the beauty hidden before our eyes. He also writes poems. His goal in life is to see God.

PAIGE MITCHELL, CENTRAL STUDENT   **SUPERINTENDENT ROBIN WHITE**   **PRINCIPAL NANCY ROUSSEAU**

Image Acknowledgements

The Publishers thank the following individuals and organizations for authorization to use their illustrations.

Cover Illustration - Rachel Gibson

Title Page – Photography by Kirk Jordan.

Dedication – Little Rock Nine Congressional Gold Medal by US Mint. Public Domain.

Page vii ....Photo courtesy of Sybil Jordan Hampton. viii Photo by Eurydice Stanley.

Page ix ....Photograph by Kirk Jordan. x Photograph by Eurydice Stanley

Page 2 ....Graphic illustration by Rachel Gibson

Page 4 ....Segregated water cooler by Russell Lee. Farm Security Administration. 1939. Public Domain.

Page 5 ....Photograph by Eurydice Stanley.

Page 6 ....Graphic illustration by Rachel Gibson.

Page 8 ....Will Counts Collection: Indiana University Archives.

Page 10 ....Photograph courtesy of Elizabeth Eckford

Page 12 ....Photograph courtesy of Elizabeth Eckford.

Page 14 ....2005 Black History Month Stamp Set by U.S. Postal Service.

Page 16-17 .Display courtesy of the National Park Service Little Rock Central High School NHS.

Page 18 ....Graphic illustration by Rachel Gibson.

Page 20 ....Will Counts Collection: Indiana University Archives.

Page 22 ....Will Counts Collection: Indiana University Archives.

Page 23 ....1832 Playbill of Thomas Rice performing as the minstrel, "Jim Crow." Artist Unknown. Public Domain.

Page 24 ....Image courtesy of the National Park Service Little Rock Central High School NHS.

Page 26 ....Will Counts Collection: Indiana University Archives.

Page 28 ....Graphic illustration by Rachel Gibson.

Page 30 ....Will Counts Collection: Indiana University Archives.

Page 31 ....Will Counts Collection: Indiana University Archives.

Page 32 ....Image by Will Counts courtesy Arkansas Democrat – Gazette.

Page 34 ....Will Counts Collection: Indiana University Archives

Page 36 ....Graphic Illustration by Rachel Gibson.

Page 38 ....Photo courtesy of the National Park Service Little Rock Central High School NHS.

Page 40 ...."A Long Walk" by former student Sophie King. Courtesy of Little Rock Central High School.

Page 42 ....Will Counts Collection: Indiana University Archives.

Page 43 ....Photograph by Eurydice Stanley. Display Courtesy of Arkansas National Guard Museum.

Page 44 ...."Testament" by former student John Deering. Courtesy of Little Rock Central High School.

Page 46 ....Will Counts Collection: Indiana University Archives.

Page 48 ....Document courtesy of the President Dwight D. Eisenhower Presidential Library.

Page 50 ....Image courtesy of the President Dwight D. Eisenhower Presidential Library.

Page 52 ....Photograph by Kirk Jordan.

Page 54 ....Photograph by Will Counts courtesy Arkansas Democrat – Gazette.

Page 56 ....Graphic illustration by Rachel Gibson.

Page 58 ....Photograph courtesy of Arkansas Democrat-Gazette.

Page 60 ....Graphic Illustration by Rachel Gibson.

Page 62 ....Arkansas Democrat – Gazette photograph.

Page 64 ....Little Rock Central High School Tiger newspaper photograph courtesy of Little Rock Central High.

Page 66 ....Arkansas Gazette-Democrat photograph.

Page 67 ....Little Rock Central High School Tiger photograph courtesy of Little Rock Central High.

Page 68 ....Graphic Illustration by Rachel Gibson.

Page 70 ....Artwork by Nancy Wilson courtesy of Little Rock Central High.

Elizabeth Eckford's Notes

There are numerous books available at the Little Rock Central High School National Historic Park Service that provide first-person accounts of student experiences at Central. I encourage you to visit the Park Service website to learn more about the Central High Crisis https://www.nps.gov/chsc/index.htm and visit the bookstore online. Here are some additional thoughts about specific passages in the book.

1   I was moved by the diligence of the citizens of Montgomery who refused to ride public transport for more than a year during the Montgomery Bus Boycott.

2   Several books have been written regarding the use and abuse of African Americans as if they were subhuman, especially in the medical field. The Immortal Life of Henrietta Lacks by Rebecca Skloot is a recommended read. The movie, Miss Evers' Boys, addresses the unethical Tuskegee experiment which withheld treatment from patients to study the impact of their symptoms without the participant's informed consent.

3   Orval Faubus' book, *Down from The Hills* features many political cartoons that lambast his decisions as Governor. Commentary includes dissenting opinions regarding his decisions and actions while leading the state of Arkansas.

4   President Eisenhower's address can be viewed at https://www.c-span.org/video/?200504-1/dwight-d-eisenhower-presidential-library.

5   Counts later wrote a book titled A Life is More than a Moment: The Desegregation of Little Rock's Central High in 1999. He passed away two years later. He was very proud of bringing Hazel and me back together for the Reconciliation poster. His poster remains very successful and has sold many copies.

6   David Margolick wrote Elizabeth and Hazel: Two Women of Little Rock in 2011 after publishing an article on the website of Vanity Fair in 2007 commemorating the 50th anniversary of the desegregation of Central High. His book recounts the details of our fateful interaction in 1957 and our subsequent lives.

7   Senator Lewis has been a champion of civil rights who ascended from serving as the Chairman of the Student Nonviolent Coordinating Committee (SNCC) to Congress. He has served the people of Georgia and the United States for forty years as a member of the U.S House of Representatives. Learn more about his contributions by reading Freedom Riders: John Lewis and Jim Zwerg on the Front Lines of the Civil Rights Movement by Ann Bausum. You can learn about other young civil rights leaders whose efforts were critical to the movement by reading The Shadows of Youth: The Remarkable Journey of the Civil Rights Generation by Andrew B. Lewis.

Dates that Shaped Elizabeth's Life

May 17, 1954 – Brown v. Board of Education Supreme Court case rules school segregation unconstitutional.

May 24, 1955 – The "Blossom Plan" is approved, authorizing the gradual integration of black students.

May 31, 1955 – The Supreme Court rules desegregation must take place "with all deliberate speed" in Brown II.

August 28, 1955 – Fourteen-year old Emmett Till is brutally murdered in Money, Mississippi for allegedly flirting with a white woman. His mother Mamie displays his body for the world to see.

December 1, 1955 – Rosa Parks is arrested in Montgomery, Alabama, for refusing to give her seat to a white man. Her arrest sparks the year-long Montgomery Bus Boycott, led by Dr. Martin Luther King, Jr.

March 11, 1956 – One hundred U.S. Senators and U.S. Representatives protest the Brown ruling by signing The Southern Manifesto, demanding the Supreme Court decision be reversed.

August 31, 1957 – Federal Judge Ronald Davies rules in favor of Central High integration.

September 2, 1957 – Governor Orval Faubus predicts during a state Labor Day address, "Blood will run through the streets" if black students attempt to attend Central. He deploys the Arkansas National Guard to Central High.

September 3, 1957 – First day of school at Central for white students. African American students are asked to stay home to prevent conflict.

September 4, 1957 – Elizabeth's first day of school. She and the Little Rock Nine were blocked from entering the building. Photographs were captured of Elizabeth's attack while encircled by an enraged mob.

September 5, 1957 – Images of Elizabeth's attack make international news. The world begins to watch the Central High Crisis. The Little Rock Nine study outside of school awaiting the ruling of the court.

September 23, 1957 – The Little Rock Nine enter Central through a side door and attend school for a few hours before being forced to leave protected by police. Outside, incensed segregationists brutally beat African American journalist Alex Wilson.

September 24, 1957 – Little Rock Mayor requests President Dwight D. Eisenhower to send military troops to maintain order.

September 24, 1957 – In a national address, President Dwight D. Eisenhower advises the country he is deploying the 101st Airborne Division to ensure the Little Rock Nine's safe passage. He federalizes the Arkansas National Guard under proclamation 3204.

September 25, 1957 – The Little Rock Nine are escorted into Central High under armed guard.

November 1957 – The 101st withdraws and the federalized Arkansas National Guard assumes the role of protecting the Little Rock Nine. Their security is lacking. The Nine endure constant attacks.

December 17, 1957 - Minnijean Brown is suspended for dropping chili on another student after being tripped in the cafeteria.

February 6, 1957 – Minnijean Brown is expelled from Central despite enduring two separate attacks.

May 27, 1958 – Ernest Green becomes the first African American Central High graduate. Dr. Martin Luther King, Jr. attends his ceremony.

September 12, 1958 – Cooper v. Aaron rules the states are bound by the decisions of the Supreme Court even if they disagree.

September 27, 1958 – Little Rock public high schools are closed.

1958-1959 – The "Lost Year." Students homeschooled, attended private schools, or went started employment early. Governor Faubus closed Little Rock high schools to prevent desegregation.

August 12, 1959 – Public high schools reopen in Little Rock, Arkansas. Five African American students enroll at Central High including two original members of the Little Rock Nine.

August 28, 1963 – Dr. Martin Luther King, Jr. delivers his powerful "I Have a Dream" speech at the March on Washington for Jobs and Freedom in Washington, DC.

November 22, 1963 – President John F. Kennedy is assassinated in Dallas, Texas.

September 15, 1963 – The 16th Street Baptist Church is bombed in protest to school desegregation, killing Cynthia Wesley (14), Carole Robertson (14), Addie Mae Collins (14) and Denise McNair (11).

July 2, 1964 – The Civil Rights Act of 1964 is signed into law by President Lyndon B. Johnson. Title VII bans discrimination based on race, color, religion, sex, or national origin.

Dates that Shaped Elizabeth's Life

March 7, 1965 – More than 600 nonviolent marchers are beaten by state troopers while protesting for voting rights in Selma, Alabama. Jimmy Lee Jackson's subsequent death is a major impetus during the Civil Rights Movement.

August 6, 1965 – President Lyndon Johnson signs the Voter's Right Act outlawing discriminatory voting practices.

October 2, 1967 – Thurgood Marshall is sworn in as the first African American Supreme Court Justice.

April 4, 1968 – Dr. Martin Luther King, Jr. is assassinated. Riots erupt in more than 100 cities nationwide as a shocked nation grieves.

September 1972 – Full integration is finally achieved in Little Rock schools.

September 25, 1997 – The first city-wide recognition of the desegregation of Central High commemorates the 40th anniversary. Elizabeth is reunited with Kendall Reinhardt and Ann Williams, her only white allies as a student. Thanking them sparks her desire to share her story. Will Counts reunites Elizabeth and Hazel for a poster titled "Reconciliation."

November 9, 1999 – The Little Rock Nine are awarded the Congressional Gold Medal by President William J. Clinton.

February 16, 2001 – The Arkansas House designates the third Monday in February as the Daisy Bates Holiday in Arkansas in conjunction with the Washington federal holiday.

August 27, 2005 – The U.S. Postal Service issues 1957 Little Rock Nine postage stamp in the To Form a More Perfect Union Civil Rights movement commemorative series.

May 15, 2007 – The United States Mint issues Little Rock Silver Dollar.

September 25, 2007 – The City of Little Rock celebrates the 50th anniversary of the desegregation of Central High with elaborate city-wide celebrations. The Little Rock Central High National Historic Site is dedicated and the Nine are reunited with many of their former 101st Airborne bodyguards.

September 20, 2017 – Elizabeth makes a triumphant return to Central High to introduce her first book, The Worst First Day. Her redemptive presentation is a powerful prelude to the 60th anniversary commemoration of the school's desegregation.

The Lincoln Leadership Prize
presented to
Elizabeth Eckford
May 18, 2015
by the
Abraham Lincoln Presidential Library Foundation

Enjoying Life's Next Chapter...

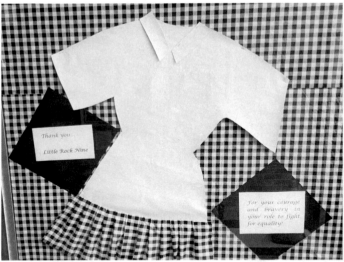